UNTAUGHT
LESSONS

UNTAUGHT LESSONS

Philip W. Jackson

Teachers College, Columbia University
New York and London

Published by Teachers College Press, 1234 Amsterdam Avenue
New York, New York

The author and publisher offer grateful acknowledgment for permission to reprint the following:

"The Schoolhouse" from *What a Kingdom it Was*, in *Selected Poems*
by Galway Kinnell (pp. 18–20). Copyright © 1982 by Galway Kinnell. Reprinted by permission of Houghton Mifflin Company. All
rights reserved.

Library of Congress Cataloging-in-Publication Data

Jackson, Philip W. (Philip Wesley), 1928–
    Untaught lessons / Philip W. Jackson.
       p.   cm.
    Includes bibliographical references and index.
    ISBN 0–8077–3194–3. — ISBN 0–8077–3193–5 (pbk.)
    1. Teaching. 2. Teachers—United States. 3. Influence
(Psychology)   I. Title.
    LB1025.3.J33   1992
    371.1'02—dc20   92–16972

ISBN 0–8077–3193–5 (pbk.)
ISBN 0–8077–3194–3

Printed on acid-free paper
Manufactured in the United States of America

99 98 97 96 95 94 93 92   8 7 6 5 4 3 2 1

TO JO

Contents

Foreword

At least since the time of Socrates, learned persons (instructed perhaps by his fate) have become increasingly unwilling to think out loud in public, to ruminate, to speculate, before their convictions are fully formed. In our day, the canons of our disciplines, empirical and otherwise, have made us all more and more adept at stacking proofs, and less and less willing to confess our bafflement at many aspects of the lives we experience and observe. In the wondrous weave of the four Sachs Lectures printed here, Philip Jackson has been so confident and brave as to speculate across and beyond the constraints we have established for ourselves, provoking us by thought and example to tread new ground in thinking about teaching and its effects on the teacher. Indeed, he invites us all, as teachers, to be ruminative and speculative about our work.

In his wide-ranging reflections on a teacher remembered, a teacher captured in poetry, a teacher observed, and the teacher in him, Phil Jackson raises more questions than he answers, making him a more gentle tutor than Socrates. It is imperative that we heed his new voice. Just as his *Life in the Classroom* unfolded the contemporary dimensions of teaching a generation ago, so today these essays suggest that we must stretch our minds mightily to invent new ways of thinking about teachers and teaching if we have any hope of meeting the unprecedented expectations that society projects upon us for the success of our schools. This rethinking will, to be sure, produce new, disciplined inquiries and insights; but it must also reaffirm that which is at the foundation of Phil Jackson's thought: that teaching is grounded in faith and hope and always surpasses our full understanding.

P. Michael Timpane

Preface

This book is about the influence teachers have on their students, though not the kind of influence that shows up on tests of achievement or other conventional measures of educational outcomes. It treats instead what we learn from our teachers about ourselves and others, and about life in general. Some of these "lessons," most of them "untaught" in the sense of not being a part of the teacher's explicit agenda or lesson plan, take the form of things we remember about our teachers long after we have bid them adieu, the qualities that endear some of them to us for a lifetime and cause others to remain objects of ridicule and scorn for just as long. It also considers the effects teachers have on us that fail to register as memories at all. Most of these effects go unacknowledged by most of us, or so we might imagine to be the case, given the absence of specific memories. Other effects arouse within us nothing save a vague sense of indebtedness and gratitude, or perhaps an involuntary shudder of distaste when a former teacher's name is casually mentioned in a conversation with friends or when we chance to think of it on our own. In either case we are often unable to explain why we continue to feel as we do.

This book also touches upon the reciprocal question of how teaching as an occupation influences those who teach. The interjection of that topic came as an afterthought, quite frankly, and consequently it gets treated rather superficially and then only in the final chapter. Nonetheless, skimpy though its treatment may be, its inclusion serves as a reminder that teachers everywhere are shaped by what goes on in their classrooms quite as directly as are their students, though differently, of course, and usually without conscious intent. The latter form of teaching's influence is seldom examined, presumably because it has little or nothing to do with the avowed purposes of schooling. But such a view is obviously shortsighted, for the effect teaching has on teachers partially determines who stays within teaching and who leaves the profession, and it indirectly affects the "untaught lessons" that teachers pass along to their students. For these reasons among others the topic remains worthy of continued attention.

The volume began as a series of three lectures—the Julius and Rosa Sachs Memorial Lectures—delivered at Teachers College in the fall of 1990. The first three chapters comprise the text of what was said on those occasions. The fourth and final chapter was added after the lectures were finished. My initial idea in planning the three talks was to explore from multiple perspectives the influence teachers have on their students. To fulfill that goal I decided to examine my memories of one of my own teachers (my high school teacher of algebra), to look at how a poet (Galway Kinnell) dealt with the subject of an adult revisiting his old school, and to report on a set of observations I had recently made of a teacher in action (a first grade teacher in a Chicago public school). My hope was that each of these three outlooks would highlight something special about the ways in which teachers leave their mark on those they teach.

I had another goal as well. I wanted to demonstrate the value of using personal recollections and works of art as sources of insight into the nature of teaching and its effects. Within today's educational research community the study of teaching is largely confined, methodologically, to observational studies of teachers in action or to interviews of teachers in which the latter are questioned about their ways of working and (less frequently) about the reasons behind what they do. Such studies are obviously of value, which is why I chose to devote one of my three lectures to direct classroom observations (though my own manner of observing in this particular case was much less structured and more freewheeling than is common in most observational studies). Notwithstanding the importance of what can be learned in this firsthand way, there is also value, I believe, in studies of teaching whose "data," if that's the word for it, are not immediately visible to the eye or audible to the ear and therefore might be called "secondhand" to contrast with what can be seen or heard on the spot. My two favorite examples of such secondhand "data" include the memories one retains of one's own teachers and the insights of artists who have chosen to reflect upon their own classroom experiences or sought to depict the work of teachers from a third-person perspective (Plato's descriptions of Socrates in action comes to mind at once as the prime example of such efforts). I wanted the Sachs lectures to instantiate my belief in the legitimacy of using such sources to explore the nature of teaching. Whether I have managed to do so successfully remains for others to decide.

Acknowledgments

Among the many people to whom I owe thanks for helping to make this book possible, none ranks above P. Michael Timpane, President of Teachers College, who invited me to deliver the Sachs Lectures and who made it possible for my wife and me to reside on campus during the semester in which they were delivered. President Timpane and his wife, Genevieve, were the perfect host and hostess throughout the months of our visit. We cannot thank them sufficiently for the many courtesies they extended to us during that time.

Many others at Teachers College added to both the physical comfort and the intellectual delight of our stay there. Nancy Griffing and Valerie Henning of the President's office went out of their way to assist me at every turn, as did Donald Underwood and Robin Eliot. Robin even managed to pull some strings that enabled me to become a late entry in the 1990 New York marathon! Rose Rudnitsky, who became my New York running partner until she suffered an injury, not only encouraged me to complete that marathon, but also helped induct me into the mores and routines of life on the third floor of Main Hall, where my office was located.

No one contributed more to making our stay personally rewarding and unforgettable than did René Arcilla and his wife Patricia Dahl. Their initial welcome made us quickly feel at home and their continued friendship enriched our visit daily. Without them neither my wife nor I would have had nearly as delightful a time as their presence made possible.

After each of the lectures and during the days that preceded and followed them I had many stimulating conversations with members of the Teachers College faculty who had attended one or more of my talks or with whom I shared some special interest. The outcome of those conversations seldom led to changes in the lectures themselves, but they were encouraging all the same and they often generated ideas that I continue to think about and draw upon these many months later. At the risk of overlooking some of those conversational companions, I must acknowledge with gratitude the lively and memorable exchanges I had with Professors René Arcilla, Lois Bloom, Judith Burton, Lambros Comitas, Linda Darling-Hammond, Celia Genishi, Joseph Grannis, Maxine Greene, Ellen Lagemann, Hope Leichter, Dale Mann, Robert McClintock, Harry Passow, Stephen Thornton, Richard Wolf, and Karen Zumwalt. Each responded to me as to an esteemed colleague, making me feel a part of the vibrant intellectual community within Teachers College.

Carole Saltz, the Director of Teachers College Press, not only attended all three of my Sachs lectures and offered to publish them, she also shared with me her detailed and insightful reactions to their contents. Every author should be blessed with as loyal and dedicated an editor!

It almost goes without saying that I am grateful to Mrs. Theresa Henzi for having been my algebra teacher those many years ago and to "Mrs. Martin" (a pseudonym) for allowing me, much more recently, to be a frequent visitor to her first grade classroom. Each taught me more than they knew they were teaching, I am sure, a condition that I have found to characterize teachers in general. I also thank Harcourt Brace Jovanovich for allowing me to reproduce Galway Kinnell's poem, "The Schoolhouse."

Back home in Chicago, where I initially drafted the lectures and later prepared them for publication, I was helped by the candid comments of my two research assistants, Robert Boostrom and David Hansen, and by the unflagging support and encouragement of Diane Bowers, Administrative Assistant at the Benton Center for Curriculum and Instruction, which is part of the Department of Education at the University of Chicago.

Finally, to my wife, Jo, I owe much more than I can ever say. With utmost gratitude, I dedicate this book to her.

CHAPTER 1

B(e)aring the Traces
*Reflections on a Sense of Being
Indebted to a Former Teacher*

Mrs. Theresa Henzi was my high school algebra
teacher in Vineland, New Jersey in 1942, my freshman
year. She was a heavyset woman, shorter than average, almost dumpy in appearance, and somewhat dowdy in at-
tire—nondescript dresses with hems at mid-calf, modest
cameo brooch pinned to the collar, and "sensible" shoes
with low heels and laces. Her ankles were thick and she
wore rimless, octagonal glasses whose lenses reflected
light much of the time, making it difficult to read the look
in her eyes. She had a pleasant, round face framed by wavy
brown hair, streaked with grey. I would guess she must
have been in her mid- to late fifties during the year I had
her as my teacher.

What I remember most vividly about my early morning classes in Mrs. Henzi's room was the way she handled
our homework assignments. Three or four students at a
time would be sent to the blackboard at the front of the
room to work out one of the problems that had been assigned the day before. These were usually textbook exercises consisting of equations to be simplified and solved for
x. Mrs. Henzi, standing at the side of the room opposite the
windows, her glasses flashing with reflected light, would
read the problem aloud for the students at the board to
copy and solve while the rest of the class looked on. As each
student finished his calculation he would turn and face the

1

front of the room, moving slightly to one side as he did so in order to make his board work visible. Mrs. Henzi would inspect each solution carefully (as would everyone who was seated), noting not only the answer but each of the steps taken to reach it. (All of the calculations had to be displayed in detail on the board.) If everything was correct she would send the student back to his seat with a word of praise and a curt nod. If the student had made an error she would have him take a close look at his work to see if he could find his mistake. "There is something wrong there, Robert," she would say, "Take another look." If after a few seconds of scrutiny Robert was unable to detect his error, Mrs. Henzi would ask for volunteers (of which there were usually plenty) to point out where their hapless classmate had gone wrong.

The most memorable part of this daily routine usually took place in the midst of each round of blackboard calculations before even the quickest student had finished his work. It was then that Mrs. Henzi would bark a command whose occurrence became routine. Its precise timing was always unexpected, however, and she delivered it in a voice whose volume made the whole class react with a start. "KEEP YOUR WITS ABOUT YOU!" she would thunder. One was seldom sure at first to whom those words were directed, if to anyone in particular. Often they sounded as though they were meant for us all. But at other times the direction of Mrs. Henzi's gaze made it apparent that she had detected an error in the making and was warning its would-be-perpetrator that he or she was about to go wrong and was headed for an algebraic waterloo. Because it was not always clear which of these was so, the effect of each outburst, in addition to startling everyone, was to make those of us in our seats scrutinize the board work with renewed fervor, searching for the error that Mrs. Henzi with her X-ray eyes seemed to have caught almost before it happened.

The students at the board did not always gain in alertness in response to these unexpected admonitions. Sometimes one or more of them, each convinced that he or she was the target of Mrs. Henzi's outburst, would go back to check on calculations already completed and in the process become so flustered that they would wind up adding mistakes where there had been none. Even if they could find no errors in their previous work, they would sometimes persist in their search for quite some time before moving on from where they had left off, having wasted a goodly amount of time in the process. On the whole, however, Mrs. Henzi's command had a positive effect. With every refrain of "KEEP YOUR WITS ABOUT YOU!" the class as a whole grew more attentive.

The remainder of what took place during that year in Mrs. Henzi's algebra class is mostly a blur to me now. I recall doing a fair amount of seatwork and I think we were given weekly quizzes on Fridays, but that's about it insofar as my memory of specific events is concerned. Oddly enough, I do not retain any visual memory of Mrs. Henzi in the act of what today is sometimes referred to as "frontal teaching," which is to say, standing in the front of the room, chalk in hand, giving direct instruction about how to do this or that. I try to picture her in that posture, which I am sure she must have adopted on countless occasions, but all I come up with is the image of her standing at the side of the room supervising our daily review of homework, her octagonal eyeglasses flashing like twin mirrors with reflected light. At the same time I can easily recall a fair amount of the academic substance of what went on that year. I remember several of the rules we used to solve equations, for example. In those days that was the way algebra was taught or at least that was the way we learned it. No effort was made to equip us with the kind of understanding sought by today's teachers of mathematics. We learned to solve equations, period. And the way one did that was by applying rules. "Collect like terms," "Find the lowest common denominator," "Remove the parentheses," "Change signs when you change sides," were a few of these rules. Such maxims were easy enough to remember and the nice thing was, they worked. One never bothered to ask

why. What was important was to "solve for x", and so long
as one came up with the right answer, who cared about
underlying principles? Years later, when I got to college, I
began to understand why some of those rules I had learned
back in high school worked as well as they did. But
throughout my stay in Mrs. Henzi's class, algebra was like
a car that one could drive without knowing anything at all
about what went on under the hood.

Within the space of a few months I managed to become
a pretty good driver of Mrs. Henzi's "solve-for-x" machine.
I finished the year with straight A's in algebra and, more
importantly, came away from the experience with a firm
desire to move ahead in mathematics. (That desire was
temporarily squelched the following year, sad to say, but
the story behind that quirk of fate need not concern us
here, save to mention that retrospectively I blame it on bad
teaching.) What was Mrs. Henzi's role in contributing to
my initial success and in nurturing my desire for more
math? What else, beyond the rules of algebra, did I learn
under her tutelage? The truth is, I am not at all certain.
Mrs. Henzi was unreservedly my favorite teacher that year,
that much I do remember with clarity, and I continued to
refer to her as such for many years afterward. Indeed, even
today I would certainly number her among the most memorable teachers I have ever had. But in all honesty I am not
entirely sure why I remember her as vividly as I do, and
why I continue to think of her, these many years later, with
such a curious mixture of fondness and puzzlement. The
fact that I learned a lot of algebra that year certainly has
something to do with the fondness part; I have no doubt
about that. But I would be surprised if the explanation
stops there. Moreover, I think it would be hard to say
which came first, my liking for Mrs. Henzi or my success-
ful mastery of the material she taught. I suspect the two
were closely intertwined and I have no idea how to un-
tangle them. Yet I feel compelled to reflect on that en-
tanglement and on the overall residue of feelings asso-
ciated with my memory of Mrs. Henzi. Such matters, it

seems to me, bear upon some crucial aspects of teaching that seldom get scrutinized. They also touch upon the much more ambitious topic of how we as a nation think about our schools and their mission.

At the root of my uncertainty about how to interpret my lingering memory of Mrs. Henzi, and the mixed feelings that accompany it, lies the strong suspicion that what I learned in her class was by no means restricted to algebra. Yet at the same time, as I have already acknowledged, I cannot describe that extra learning (if that's what to call it) in the same way that I can describe my knowledge of algebra nor can I even say for sure that it actually occurred. Why then do I persist in believing that it did?

I do so in part because I know that's how human influence operates. In other domains of my life I have often had the experience of belatedly coming to realize that someone or something left its mark on me without my knowing it. Surely the same has happened to everyone else. Who has not felt compelled at one time or another to say something like, "I realize now just what so-and-so meant to me" or "I see now how much I was changed by that event?" Sometimes the dawning of our awareness occurs more casually and without the feeling of our having achieved a major insight into the forces that have formed us. We find ourselves chattering on about something and suddenly we notice that we have used an expression borrowed from a friend or relation or, even more subtly, someone makes the discovery for us. "You sounded just like your mother when you said that," our companion remarks, "And by the way, have you noticed how you chew on your lip when you are worried, just the way she did?" Such experiences usually come as a surprise. If we bother to ponder them we may be led to wonder what else we might have inherited from the same source or from others yet to be discovered. What other shaping forces have there been in our lives that we have yet to acknowledge? Do they include our near-forgotten teachers? Is Mrs. Henzi among them?

She was so serious. Or at least that's how I remember

her. *Algebra* was certainly no joke. In fact, there were no jokes of any kind in her class. What could be funny about solving for *x*? Jokes happened in the hall outside or on the bus on the way to school. Sometimes their remnants were smuggled into class and passed from desk to desk or telegraphed across the room via a none-too-subtle network of winks, whispers, and smirks. But those exchanges seldom lasted long. We soon settled down to the business at hand. "Esther, Raymond, Paul, and Phyllis. To the board, please," she would say. And off the four of them would go while all the rest of us, save a few eager beavers, breathed a sigh of relief and thanked our lucky stars that we had been spared the unyielding scrutiny of Mrs. Henzi's discerning eye for at least the first round. Our turns would come soon enough.

Is that what she taught us, to be serious about algebra? Or did algebra teach us that? She certainly reinforced its teaching, if it did. There was no fooling around in her class. No pretending you knew the answer when you didn't. And of course that was the beautiful part of the subject, or so it seemed to me at the time. There always was an answer, and a correct one at that. Everything was so impartial. It didn't matter who you were or how neatly you wrote on the board or how winningly you smiled when you turned to face the teacher. The result was there for all to see: *x* = 6. Right? Or wrong? It had to be one or the other. No ifs, ands, or buts about it. Was that among the lessons taught between the lines? Perhaps so, but it's hard to understand why that lesson should strike with any greater force in an algebra class than in, say, first grade arithmetic. The fact that two and two always equal four and never five teaches us fully as much about the precision and impartiality of numbers as does any algebra lesson. Or so it would seem.

Perhaps a more crucial insight had something to do with the realization that difficult things can become easy if you master them a step at a time. For we certainly learned that, too, in Mrs. Henzi's class. Our mastery of algebra chugged ahead slowly and steadily, like a train on a gradually ascending track. There was little huff and puff and the incline was barely noticeable. But miss a day or two and WHAM!: The road to recovery tilted upward at an angle that made one's heart pound. As a result, few of us missed class if we could help it, and if we did we tried to get the homework assignment from one of our classmates, along with an explanation of how to solve the ever-more-complicated set of equations.

As I settled down to my studies after school, algebra usually came first. I don't remember now whether it was more satisfying to complete than were assignments in my other school subjects, or whether I was simply more fear-ful of what would happen if I didn't get it done, but I do recall that it was not a good idea to skip algebra, no matter what else might have to be left undone. Do I credit or blame Mrs. Henzi for so ordering my priorities? To some extent, certainly. Did the habit of seldom failing to do my algebra assignment transfer to other school subjects and possibly even to life in general? Who knows? Algebra was certainly not the only subject in which I did homework dutifully. What mark if any did the dutiful completion of all those assignments leave on my character? How can one answer such a question? Why might one want to do so? What difference does it make?

Wittgenstein's *Tractatus* closes with the lines: "Wovon man nicht sprechen kann, darüber muß man schweigen" (What we cannot speak about we must pass over in si-lence). That sounds like good advice. Perhaps we should take it to heart when addressing the likes of a Mrs. Henzi and her real or imagined influence. Since we are unable to speak of that influence with anything like certainty, why not leave it be, pass over it in silence?

Of course, that is precisely what we do most of the time. How often do we think about the differences, if any, such teachers may have made in our lives? How often do teachers themselves think in those terms? Not very often would be my guess. Indeed, I suspect most adults barely recall the names of many of the teachers they have had over their lifetimes, much less are they able to pinpoint what those now nameless mentors may have done for them or to them during the months or perhaps even years of their tutelage. Oh, there are notable exceptions of course. Some people may remember every teacher they have ever had and perhaps we can all recall the exceptional teacher or two (or more if we were lucky), the ones who made, as we say, "a real difference in our lives" and who may have done so with such dramatic suddenness that we can still recount the specific event or remember the exact words that made the difference. But of the average, run-of-the-mill teachers, the ones whose names we may have forgotten, what is there to say save that "we had them" for this or that subject or this or that grade and that's about it?

Is it much different however with the remainder? Mrs. Henzi was surely one of those memorable teachers that most of us have a few of if we are lucky, yet when I search today for signs of her influence I am unable to say for certain what I owe her, if anything. All I come up with is the silly business about how she used to shout "KEEP YOUR WITS ABOUT YOU!" when students were doing their homework assignments at the board. What shall we make of this? Shall we treat it as evidence of my failing memory or is it possible that I have been kidding myself all of these years and that Mrs. Henzi has played no greater role in my life than Miss What's-her-name, who taught sophomore English in the same high school, or Mr. Something-stein, who taught physics?

I am certainly willing to entertain the possibility that I have been deluding myself all this time, indulging in a form of sentimentality that is decidedly old-fashioned, one that I should by now have outgrown, but before relegating Mrs. Henzi to the list of teachers whose names I can no longer remember, I am compelled by a philosophical work that I read recently to try a different tack. To do so I need back away from my recollections of Mrs. Henzi and my thoughts about them at least far enough to make visible their resemblance to a well-known and historically significant phenomenon with which every educated adult is at least casually familiar. I refer to the tradition of skepticism that surfaces recurrently within the history of philosophy and has done so for millennia.

Within what is called "modern philosophy" Descartes is the person we most readily associate with skepticism as a point of view. His "cogito ergo sum" is known by every schoolboy to have been the famous Frenchman's ultimate defense against the insidious encroachment of an all-consuming doubt. But skepticism hardly ended with Descartes. In one form or another it has continued to trouble the sleep of almost every major philosopher from his day to ours. Moreover, as a kind of psychic ailment it is by no means restricted to philosophers. Variations of it have been known to attack literary critics, political analysts, and artists of all kinds. Today's deconstructionists are among its most recent victims, the focus of their doubt being the meaning attached to words. Moreover, skepticism has a way not only of spilling over its boundaries and invading other domains of human thought but of spreading like wildfire wherever it may happen to catch hold.

Commenting on this unruliness as it pertains to the eruption of irony (a form of skepticism) within literature, Paul de Man (1983) observes,

> The moment the innocence or authenticity of our sense of being in the world is put into question, a far from harmless process gets underway. It may start as a casual bit of play with a stray loose end of the fabric, but before long the entire texture of the self is unraveled and comes apart. The whole process happens at an unsettling speed. Irony possesses an inherent tendency to gain momentum and not to stop until it has run its full course; from the small and apparently innocuous [even potentially therapeutic] exposure of a small self deception it soon reaches the dimensions of the absolute. (p. 215)

Though there are many forms the skeptic's doubt has taken over the years, two of the most common within the

sphere of philosophy call into question the reality of an
external world and the existence of other minds. External-
world skepticism, which is the more radical of the two, la-
ments our incapacity to experience the world save through
the medium of our senses and, therefore, our inability to
ever have direct contact with a reality outside the self.
Other-minds skepticism is occasioned by our inability to
experience the world *of others* from any perspective save
our own, a condition that inevitably calls into question the
validity of what others tell us about their experience and
ultimately the reality of their psychic life, which is what
they seemingly report upon. This is hardly the place to offer even a textbookish overview of such an important topic
but there are two additional points about the skeptic's
position that merit the briefest of comments.

The first is that the skeptic's doubts are counterin-
tuitive. They strike most people as being an assault on
common sense. Indeed, they strike skeptics themselves
that way much of the time. Therein lies the source of both
their attraction and revulsion. On the one hand they seem
ridiculous; on the other hand, logically compelling. David
Hume (1969 [1739]) once commented memorably on what
skeptical thinking did to him and how he coped with it.
Such thoughts, he said,

> [have] so wrought upon me, and heated my brain, that
> I am ready to reject all belief and reasoning, and can
> look upon no opinion even as more probable or likely
> than another. Where am I, or what? From what causes
> do I derive my existence, and to what condition shall I
> return? Whose favour shall I court, and whose anger
> must I dread? What beings surround me? and on whom
> have I any influence, or who have any influence on me?
> I am confounded with all these questions, and begin to
> fancy myself in the most deplorable condition imagin-
> able, inviron'd with the deepest darkness, and utterly
> depriv'd of the use of every member and faculty.
>
> Most fortunately it happens, that since reason is in-
> capable of dispelling these clouds, nature herself suf-

fices to that purpose, and cures me of this philosophical melancholy and delirium, either by relaxing this bent of mind, or by some avocation, and lively impression of my senses, which obliterate all these chimeras. I dine, I play a game of backgammon, I converse, and am merry with my friends; and when after three of four hour's amusement, I wou'd return to these speculations, they appear so cold, and strain'd, and ridiculous, that I cannot find in my heart to enter into them any farther. (p. 316)

So much for Hume's celebrated cure, a surefire remedy for those who love backgammon, I suppose. Others have sought to dispel similar doubts, whether their own or those of skeptics with whom they were conversing, by kicking stones or pinching themselves or sticking their hand in front of their disputant's nose and shouting, "See!" In short, the natural urge seems to be to shake free of such misgivings long before they catch hold or, if already caught within their grip, to do so as soon as circumstances allow. As Hume's example makes clear, the proximity of a friendly pub has been known to help.

A second point to make about skepticism as a philosophical position is that what the skeptic calls into doubt is not our *belief* about an external world or the minds of others but our *knowledge* that such things exist. The doubt, in other words, is fundamentally epistemological. It is not an expression of uncertainty about the way we would *like* things to be or how they *seem* to us. Rather, it has to do with claims about reality and the grounds of our acquaintance with it.

Among the many efforts to dispel the skeptic's doubts, one very recent solution comes from Stanley Cavell, the Harvard philosopher whose writings probe the relationship between philosophy and literature. It was Cavell's notions that got me thinking about a possible connection between my own misgivings about Mrs. Henzi's influence and those classic doubts that have troubled philosophers over the ages. This is hardly the place to undertake an exposition of Cavell's handling of the question of skepticism, which turns out to be the pivotal issue in all of his writings, but I do need to say a word or two about the general drift of his argument.

In essence, Cavell recommends that we abandon efforts to refute radical skepticism once and for all. He invites us instead to learn to live with the recurrent doubts that periodically trigger the skeptic's angst. At the same time he offers an interpretation of those doubts that seeks to identify what might be called their pathological nature, an interpretation too complicated, unfortunately, to go into at this point. What we must give up, Cavell goes on to insist, is the idea of unimpeachable knowledge. Both kinds of skepticism, in his view, make unreasonable demands. "[S]ince we cannot know the world exists," he contends, "its presentness to us cannot be a function of knowing. The world is to be *accepted;* as the presence of other minds is not to be known, but acknowledged" (Cavell, 1976, p. 324).

Accept the world and acknowledge the presence of others. That is the essence of Cavell's advice. How does one accomplish that? By acting responsibly, by openly expressing one's sense of relatedness to others. "Mightn't it be" Cavell (1979) rhetorically inquires,

> that just this haphazard, unsponsored state of the world, just this radiation of relationships, of my cares and commitments, provides the milieu in which my knowledge of others can best be expressed? Just *this*— say expecting someone to tea; or returning a favor; waving goodbye; reluctantly or happily laying in the groceries for a friend with a cold; feeling rebuked, and feeling it would be humiliating to admit the feeling; pretending not to understand that the other has taken my expression, with a certain justice, as meaning more than I sincerely wished it to mean; hiding inside a marriage; hiding outside a marriage—just such things are perhaps the most that knowing others comes to, or has come to for me. (p. 439)

Michael Fischer (1989), a sympathetic expositor of Cavell's views, summarizes them in this way:

> The other-minds skeptic construes our distance from others in terms of ignorance, making our metaphysical finitude—our separation from others—an insoluble intellectual lack or problem (we cannot know them). While also insisting on our separateness, Cavell, by contrast, pictures it in terms of avoidance and acknowledgment, terms that insist on our responsibility to one another, our role in what joins or parts us. (p. 74)

Now it is time to draw the connection, as I see it, between philosophical skepticism in general, Cavell's attempt at a resolution of it, and my difficulty in tracing Mrs. Henzi's long-ago influence on me. First, I must hasten to disavow any intellectual pretensions that might erroneously be read into my rough and ready treatment of philosophical skepticism. It would be downright silly of me to pretend that my doubts about Mrs. Henzi's influence are even remotely equivalent in either philosophical importance or psychological gravity to, say, Descartes's persistent search for an epistemological bedrock or David Hume's ambitious struggle to extend the province of Newtonian rationality. What is similar, however, between the skeptic's posture and my own is the shared wish to be certain about something, to *know* it rather than simply *believe* it, combined with the gnawing suspicion that the enterprise of seeking that knowledge is fundamentally misguided, that it represents not only an affront to common sense but is downright pernicious in its long-term effect.

Are those shared suspicions justified? They certainly seem to be so in the case of the skeptic's doubts about the existence of an external world or the presence of other minds. But what about something as commonplace as the search for concrete evidence of a former teacher's influence? What makes such an effort misguided? Why should it have pernicious effects? What turns out to be misguided about it, in my opinion, is not the pondering per se, but the direction such reflection takes when the call for hard-nosed evidence is introduced. Moreover, it is the insistence upon *being sure* about such matters, which is analogous to the skeptic's demand for certainty, that has or can have pernicious effects.

Here is where Cavell's recommended solution to the skeptic's doubts comes into play. His rejection of the skeptic's search for knowledge leads me to wonder whether my demand for hard evidence and for proof in such matters is also unreasonable, in addition, that is, to its being impossible to satisfy. He encourages me to trust what I believe, to *accept* my feelings of indebtedness to Mrs. Henzi and to *acknowledge* them by means other than a search for the traces of her legacy to me. By what other means? By acts of gratitude perhaps. A letter to Mrs. Henzi's children, if she had any, might be one such gesture. By committing myself to trying to be a positive influence in the lives of my own students.

(A fantasy intrudes. For some reason the possibility of my carrying on the good work of my former teacher, and doing so in her honor, calls to mind the sentimental pledge made to the bedridden Ronald Reagan in *The Knute Rockne Story*—"This one's for the Gipper." In like manner I picture myself pausing momentarily outside the classroom. "This one's for you, Mrs. Henzi," I whisper with closed eyes, as I turn the knob on the door. But of course I could never act that way. My fantasy is an expression of cynicism. Where does such a cynical view come from? Is it our old friend Skepticism speaking in a different voice? I fear so.)

Returning to more sober reflections, perhaps the most effective way of my acting on my responsibility in such matters is by continuing to ponder what it was Mrs. Henzi gave me, as I'm doing now. Perhaps if enough of us engage in that kind of endeavor we will come to a better understanding of what all teachers, for better or for worse, do for or to their students. Such at least is my hope, and my reason for spending all this time on such a remote and personal set of memories.

The kind of pondering I have in mind need not entail a search for hard evidence, though neither does it seek to ignore such evidence as might exist. It's more like coming to appreciate something, coming to realize its significance. "Realize," that sounds more like it. What does it mean to realize something? "To make real," Webster's says, "to convert from the imaginary or fictitious into the actual." Also, "[t]o cause to seem real; to impress upon the mind as actual" (*Webster's New International*, 1937, p. 2072). It is that conversion from the imaginary or fictitious to the actual, that causing "to seem real," that strikes me as being the crux of the matter. How does that happen? What causes such things as one person's influence upon another to seem real? Can that only occur through the garnering of evidence?

I have already said that I think not and offered as my own answer to the question of what makes such things real the single word: pondering. Another name for the same process might be: rumination. Doubtless there are others.

How does the process work? Well, take Mrs. Henzi, for instance. By thinking about her influence, by pondering it, I have in a sense revitalized it. I have contributed to its becoming real, at least for me. I have begun more fully to *realize*, in the root meaning of that term, what she did for me. What it feels like to engage in the process cannot be described in a few words. No metaphor that I know of captures it fully. It is sort of like searching for an object and then finding it, but not quite. It also resembles discovering something unexpectedly, but that's not it either. It's certainly not like taking something out of a trunk or digging up a treasure chest. It's more like constructing a treehouse from materials randomly strewn about the yard and the adjoining lots, a process requiring no small amount of ingenuity and imagination, if my memory serves me well. The result may not be waterproof and certainly not inhab-

itable in all seasons but it's up there, by gosh!, and up there
to stay, that's for sure. Witness the squirrels and the birds,
who peck on its roof with curiosity and cautiously explore
its interior.

There are risks in such an undertaking, as we have
seen. One is the risk of failure, which is the same as the risk
of becoming a skeptic, of having one's initial sense of indebtedness, of the kind I feel toward Mrs. Henzi, dissolve
before one's eyes. There is also a risk on the other side of
course. It is that of making up something that is absolutely
false and treating it as though it were true, building a
castle in the sky rather than a treehouse. The latter risk is
the ancient one of self-delusion.

There we have it: skeptical doubt on the one hand and
self-delusion on the other, the Scylla and Charybdis of the
kind of constructive undertaking I am advocating. Are
these two risks equal and opposite? Can one avoid them
both?

On the question of their equality it would seem to me
that when the orienting attitude is one of gratitude and
affection, as it is in the present case, the risk of giving it up
has greater costs and more negative consequences in both
psychological and social terms than does the corresponding risk of believing what is false. Far better, therefore,
that I continue to think kindly of Mrs. Henzi, even if I ex-
aggerate what she did for me, than that I abandon all
thoughts of her. Why is it far better? Simply because living
in a world where people think well of others, even if unde-
servedly sometimes, turns out to be more desirable than
living in a world where they do not.

But even if self-delusion in such matters is preferable
to skepticism, what about the possibility of avoiding both?
Sad to say, the outlook is not very promising. If, as Cavell
insists, skepticism cannot be refuted conclusively, the
temptation to become ensnared within its web of doubt
will always be a danger. Scylla, the legendary monster
who menaced seafarers of old, will never depart her rock,
at least not so long as we humans are among the passersby.

There is not much we can do about that condition, Cavell goes on to suggest, save struggle with its consequences. The seeds of doubt lie deeply embedded within our bones.

John Dewey (1929) came to much the same conclusion in his book, *The Quest for Certainty,* as readers of that work will readily recall, though he stopped short of calling the skeptic's ailment incurable. "Man who lives in a world of hazards is compelled to seek for security," Dewey announced at the start (p. 3). There are two ways of doing that, he went on to say. One is by "changing the world through action"; the other is by "changing the self in emotion and idea" (p. 3). Dewey chose the way of action, and he advocated that others do the same. But either way, even in Dewey's optimistic view, we are portrayed as almost invariably aspiring to greater security, to a firmer foundation for our doings and undergoings, as he called them, than human efforts can possibly provide. What this means, in other words, is that our hankering for certainty remains close to unquenchable, which leaves the door to skepticism continually ajar.

And what of self-delusion? Can that ever be avoided completely? Having said no to the possibility of shooing Scylla from her rocky perch, we have indirectly answered the question with respect to the whirlpool of Charybdis. For if doubt is the condition we must live with, it has to include the risk of deluding ourselves from time to time. Like the errors of Type I and Type II that statisticians speak of, the two kinds of risk are reciprocally related. As one increases, the other correspondingly decreases, though neither ever disappears completely.

I have already revealed my personal bias when it comes to thinking about the positive effects teachers may have in our lives. When in doubt with respect to those effects, as we must always be to some extent, give the benefit of that doubt to the teacher in question. That seems to me a sensible rule of thumb. It resembles the attitude of good will that undergirds our legal system, making it mandatory to consider a person innocent until proved guilty. But within our legal system such good will is only preliminary, as we all know. It precedes the execution of justice. It is meant to cover the period of indecision during which legal proceedings are underway and before the jury has announced its verdict.

What of teaching? Should the same apply there? Well, yes, of course. We should always be prepared to abandon our trust in others, teachers included, when contrary convictions become strong enough. However, when we set about judging teachers, our good will is not usually offset by a corresponding aura of suspicion and accusation which threatens to win the day and thus make a mockery of our initial kindliness. Teaching, after all, is a profession in which the practitioners, in the main, are bent on doing good. This doesn't mean that all succeed in doing so, obviously enough, but it does imply that a search for the good they do need not be plagued, at least not early on, by the threat of a guilty verdict.

Back to Mrs. Henzi for a final time. The light from those octagonal glasses of hers continues to flash in my mind's eye like an intermittent beacon whose source is now light years away. What shall I make of their distant glitter? Is there a message contained in those dots and dashes? Do they spell out KEEP YOUR WITS ABOUT YOU, PHILIP!? That would be quite appropriate, of course. Equally so would be something about getting my bearings or at least getting them straight.

I *bear* traces of my year spent with Mrs. Henzi. That much by now should be abundantly clear. Yet when I seek to *bare* those traces, to say what they are, to make them evident for all to see, I find myself unable to do so in a way that would convince the skeptic, including, as I must now acknowledge in the light of all that's been said, the skeptic in me. What makes this inability important, what ties it to the enterprise of education writ large, is that it is not mine alone. We all share it, students, parents, citizens at large, even teachers themselves—indeed, maybe teachers more than others, who knows? We all at some level are convinced that teaching makes a difference, often a huge difference in students' lives, and does so in some of the ways I have been trying to spell out here. Yet we often have a hard time convincing others of that fact. As a result, when it comes time to talk about how effectively our schools are functioning or how well a particular group of teachers are doing their job we seem to forget what we know from personal experience and we wind up relying on evidence, such as achievement test scores, that completely ignores almost everything I have been talking about and alluding to here. Perhaps there is no other way to go when our unit of concern becomes the schools of an entire city or state, or when we seek to develop tests of teacher competency to be used nationwide. But the fact (if it is one) that in such circumstances we must so limit our perspective as to rule out consideration of much of the good that teachers actually do (and maybe much of the evil as well) does not lessen by one jot or tittle the terrible danger of so doing.

If in the years ahead we cannot think more deeply than we are doing today about some of the complexities that lie at the heart of teaching, if we cannot come to appreciate more fully the role teachers can and do play in our lives, then we are doomed to having the kinds of schools and the kinds of teachers whose formative potency will remain unrealized. Such is the premise whose consequences I shall continue to explore in the chapters ahead.

There. Finished at last. (I turn from the board to face the teacher.) "Is that it, Mrs. Henzi? Is that what I was supposed to have discovered? Is that the significance of the unknown in today's educational equation?" I can see her now, nodding in approval, the reflected light of a sunny day bouncing in iridescent sparkles on the ceiling, the blackboard, the floor.

CHAPTER 2

In Search of the Apple's Core

Reflections on a Poet's Teacher

The material in this chapter has a rather curious history. It began as an address I gave a few years ago at a research conference in Belgium sponsored by an international organization devoted to the study of teachers' thinking. What turned out to be curious was the contrast between the way my talk was received by those present and the way it was subsequently dealt with by the organizers of the conference. The audience seemed to like it, at least as judged by the generosity of their applause and by favorable comments from several of those in attendance who spoke to me about it afterwards. The organizers, however, reacted much less positively. They mostly refrained from comment on the day the talk was given, which gave me an early hint of their displeasure, but when the proceedings of the conference were published a year or two later I learned in full just how displeased they had been. Mine was the only paper omitted from the published record. Not only was the paper missing from the report of the proceedings but no explanation was given for its absence. No mention was made of it having been delivered. So far as the official history of the conference was concerned, I had not even been there!

What prompted the organizers' cool response and their subsequent act of censorship? Had my paper really been that bad? Had I completely misread the warmth of the audience's response? Whether wisely or not, I never bothered to ask for an explanation. However, I think I can guess the reason for their action. What happened, I believe, is that my paper did not fulfill the expectations of those in charge. In a nutshell, the organizers of the conference were expecting science and I gave them art, or so they interpreted what I had to say. My talk began, you see, with a poem about teaching which I then proceeded to comment upon. I did so not to stir up trouble, as some seemed to think, but simply to make the point (which I thought to be fairly obvious, albeit frequently overlooked) that if we are truly dedicated to learning as much about teaching as possible we should be open to the idea of studying teachers wherever we find them—whether in real classrooms or imaginary (i.e., fictionalized) ones. That was it. That was the extent of my iconoclasm. To demonstrate the soundness of that generalization I read a poem aloud and then proceeded to talk about what it might mean and what its meaning might add to our understanding of teaching. I offered no "data" and no "findings," at least not as those terms are conventionally construed. But this was a *research* conference, remember, one whose goal, at least in part, was to impress its audience, which included not just researchers but also government officials and local university administrators, with just how intellectually rigorous and scientific our understanding of teaching had finally become. Then along comes this visitor from the States, an invited guest no less, and what does he do? He reads a poem, for heaven's sake! A *poem*, mind you! How intellectually disgraceful, how unscientific could one possibly be? What an embarrassment! No wonder my paper was shipped off to Siberia or run through the shredding machine or whatever one does in Belgium to get rid of unwanted words.

Well, I'm about to do it again, officialdom, so watch out! Only this time the local expectations are different, I trust, and the officials somewhat more charitable. Also, I plan to be a little clearer than before about what I think such an exercise might accomplish. Further, I have changed my mind about the substance of some of the things I said back then and about the appropriateness of the format as well. In the light of these changes, both substantive and contextual, I'm hoping to fare better this time. We'll see how it goes.

As before, the poem on which my remarks will center is by Galway Kinnell and is entitled "The Schoolhouse." It appears in his *Selected Poems* (1982). It is rather long for a lyrical work, being divided into four sections, each containing three stanzas of six lines. In brief, it relates the experience of a person of middle age or older, perhaps the poet himself, who comes upon his old schoolhouse, a one-room building, and stands there for some time reflecting on what went on in that now decrepit structure. In its overall structure the poem is almost a classic example of what M. H. Abrams calls "the Greater Romantic Lyric" (1984). Here is how he describes the genre:

> They present a determinate speaker in a particularized, and usually a localized, outdoor setting, whom we overhear as he carries on, in a fluent vernacular which rises easily to a more formal speech, a sustained colloquy, sometimes with himself or with the outer scene, but more frequently with a silent human auditor, present or absent. The speaker begins with a description of the landscape; an aspect or change of aspect in the landscape evokes a varied but integral process of memory, thought, anticipation, and feeling which remains closely intervolved with the outer scene. In the course of this meditation the lyric speaker achieves an insight, faces up to a tragic loss, comes to a moral decision, or resolves an emotional problem. Often the poem rounds upon itself to end where it began, at the outer scene, but with an altered mood and deepened understanding which is the result of the intervening meditation. (p. 76–77)

That is almost precisely what happens within Kinnell's poem, "The Schoolhouse," as we shall presently see.

The first section of the poem describes the speaker's initial reactions to his reencounter with his old school. His reflections about what went on there begin almost immediately. Here are the first three stanzas:

> I find it now, the schoolhouse by the tree,
> And through the broken door, in brown light,
> I see the benches in rows, the floor he
> Paced across, the windows where the fruit
> Took the shapes of hearts, and the leaves windled
> In the fall, and winter snowed on his head.
>
> In this wreck of a house we were taught
> Everything we imagined a man could know,
> All action, all passion, all ancient thought,
> What Socrates had got from Diotima,
> How Troilus laughed, in tears, in paradise,
> That crowns leapfrog through blood: casts of the dice.
>
> The door hangs from one hinge. Maybe the last
> Schoolboy simply forgot to lift the latch
> When he rushed out that spring, in his haste—
> Or maybe the same one, now fat and rich,
> Snowhaired in his turn, and plagued by thought,
> Broke his way in, looking for the dead light.

From an educational perspective, which will be the approach taken here, leaving to others a more literary analysis, one of the noteworthy features of this first section is the way it heralds the question that will come to dominate the poem, at least from an outsider's perspective. That question is: why should a grown man revisit the school of his childhood? From one point of view such a return journey is not at all unusual. We are used to the idea of people returning to their former schools or colleges for scheduled events like class reunions, for example, and we would not think it at all odd for someone to go there on his own, just on a whim perhaps, or possibly just to indulge in nostalgia. But the poem's speaker does not seem to be engaged in anything that frivolous. He seems to be embarked on a much more serious quest. Indeed, the four opening words, "I find it now," lead us to suspect that his search has been going on for quite some time. The urgency of the enterprise is reinforced in other ways as well. We soon learn that the speaker can readily imagine someone like himself, "snow-haired" and "plagued by thought," going so far as to break into the school by force, so desperate is his wish to return.

What are the plaguing thoughts that might propel someone on such a journey? We are not told at once but we soon do learn that our narrator was "looking for the dead light." "The dead light," a curiously powerful phrase, a mixture, one might say, of past and present, calling to mind something that was once living and is now deceased yet continues somehow to glow with life, to serve as a beacon of sorts. How might that work? How can the past continue to be illuminating? What can it reveal that is not already within the ken of our vision?

Those are ancient questions, as every educator knows. They are also familiar ones. They come up time and again whenever a teacher or some other spokesperson for our schools is called upon to defend the place of history in the curriculum. Or the place of literature, or art, or science, for that matter. For in a manner of speaking, all of the knowledge that is stored in books and films and in even more exotic depositories, like computers, or in that most exotic storage space of all—the human head—all of that stored knowledge can be thought of as a kind of dead light, a light that when switched on and directed outward remains capable of penetrating the darkest and furthest corner of ignorance.

But the light that the speaker in the poem seems to be searching for is not the kind of knowledge stored in books. He is not out to brush up on his history lessons, or his science or art either, for that matter, though all three enter the picture in the course of his pondering, as we have al-

ready seen in part and as we shall see more of in what soon
follows. The past he is ultimately seeking to uncover has
little to do directly with textbooks or treatises. It is linked
somehow with the characteristics of his former teacher.
And was not just lodged within that teacher's head, the
way factual knowledge or even technical skills might have
been, but permeated and infused all he said and did. The
heart of the mystery, in other words, has something to do
with the kind of a person this teacher was and what he did
to or for the speaker. (What I have just said about the
speaker in Kinnell's poem should bring to mind my memories of Mrs. Henzi, my old algebra teacher. The poem's
narrator and I seem puzzled by much the same question or
set of questions. We differ somewhat in the answers we
give, however, as will soon be evident, which is one reason
for presenting both viewpoints. Another is that poetry, as a
unique form of light, has its own way of illuminating. Unlike ordinary discourse, its beams spread out in many directions at once.)

Now back to the poem itself. The second section contains a surprise. The locale of the action suddenly shifts
from the scene of an old schoolhouse to that of a country
manor of some kind. We find ourselves being told a story of
an eccentric man who once lived there and of the fate that
befell his estate after he died. In brief, his empty house and
its grounds are taken over each winter by tramps, whom
the old boy once tried to befriend and who now use the site
as a haven from the cold. Here is the story in full.

> A man of letters once asked the local tramps
> To tea. No one came, and he read from Otway
> And Chatterton to the walls, and lived for months
> On tea. They padlocked the gate when he died.
> Snow, sleet, rain, the piss of tramps; and one year
> The lock snapped, the gate rasped open like a rooster.
>
> And now when the tramps wake sheeted in frost,
> They know it is time, they come here and sprawl
> At the foot of the statue of their host

Which they call "His Better Self," which he had called
"Knowledge," sometimes "Death," whose one gesture
Seems to beckon and yet remains obscure.

And boil their tea on the floor and pick fruit
In the garden where that man used to walk
Thinking of Eden and the fallen state,
And dust an apple as he had a book—
"Hey now, Porky, gie's the core," one hollers;
"Wise up, " says Pork, "They ain't gonna *be* a core."

There are several obvious parallels between what goes
on in those three stanzas and what went on in the first section. Both parts refer to abandoned buildings whose bro-
ken locks invite entry. The teacher and the eccentric country gentleman are both well read, bookish fellows, each is
a "man of letters," as the latter is actually called. The
tramps bring to mind a group of unruly students of the
kind that might have attended the old schoolhouse. Like
the poem's "snowhaired" speaker, they too seek out the
building in what might be called the winter of their lives,
when they awaken "sheeted with frost." And so it goes.
Echoes and re-echoes.

What are we to make of these parallels? Are the
teacher and "that man" one and the same person? And
what of the connection between the speaker and the
tramps? Is not the person searching for the schoolhouse a
wanderer in spiritual terms? Is he not, figuratively speaking, seeking refuge from the cold? Though it is tempting to
explore those and other possibilities in greater detail, I
shall refrain from doing so in order to focus on those por-
tions of this second section that most directly pertain to
teaching and to the relationship between teachers and
their students. This requires me to assume that all of the
resemblances I have mentioned (and others I have left out)
have been placed there purposefully and that one is not
doing violence to the spirit of the poem by combining ele-
ments that connect the two parts.

The pair of physical objects that I find most intriguing

in this second section are the statue around which the tramps sprawl when they come indoors and the apple that gets dusted off and eaten, core and all. Each is shrouded in mystery. Each begs to be interpreted symbolically.

To begin with the statue, which is obviously that of a male figure whose identity is unclear, it is described as being "of their host," meaning, presumably, the man who once owned the house (who may also be the teacher). But the "of" is ambiguous. Does it connote mere possession or something more? Was the statue simply *owned* by the host; is that what "of" means here, or is it also a likeness of its owner? The tramps call the statue "His Better Self," which would fit the notion of it being a likeness, though a flattering one perhaps. Yet the owner also had names for it. He called it "Knowledge," and sometimes "Death." Would he have attached those names to his own likeness? If so, what does that reveal about him? Does that make him fundamentally lighthearted, wryly ironic perhaps, or deeply serious, perhaps even deranged? And even if the statue bore no resemblance to him at all, why did he use two different names when referring to it? Did it depend on his mood and was he therefore a man of moods (as well as one of letters) or was it the angle from which the statue was seen that made the difference? Did it look like "Death" from one vantage point and like "Knowledge" from another? Did it resemble a scholar with his eyes closed perhaps? A dead teacher?

And what shall we make of the statue's ambiguous gesture, which "Seems to beckon and yet remains obscure"? If it were not beckoning, what might it be doing? Admonishing? Pointing to something? Or perhaps pausing in midthought, like a speaker who is thinking on his feet and is groping for the right word. And why are we told that it is the statue's "one" gesture? How could a statue have more than one? Might the emphasis on the gesture's singularity suggest that the statue is so lifelike that one might almost expect it to move, for instance, to come to life before one's very eyes? To interpret the statue as beckoning would be consonant with it being an Angel of Death, the Grim Reaper perhaps. But, then, teachers also beckon, don't they? Though they may not always gesture when doing so, they surely invite students to join them in the pursuit of knowledge. Is theirs too an invitation to the world of the dead? The image of the dead light that closed the poem's first section prompts us to think in those terms.

As these questions and conjectures reveal, even superficial reflection upon the identity of the statue and what it stands for inspires thoughts that both deepen and darken our conception of the narrator's mission and his fascination with the character of his former teacher. This is no mere nostalgia trip he is taking, that much is certain. He seeks to know something about knowledge and its place in his life, perhaps in the lives of us all. Whatever that something is, it seems as though his former teacher once held the key or appeared to do so at the time. The speaker credits him with having possessed, "Everything we imagined a man could know." Why, then, didn't the teacher impart this crucial piece of knowledge back then, during the days when the speaker sat at his feet? Or might he have done so without the young man knowing it? Isn't that how teaching sometimes works? Aren't we frequently taught lessons in our youth whose value and truth we only slowly come to understand and appreciate?

The apple mentioned in this second section introduces yet another layer of complexity to these reflections. Little need be said about the object's overall symbolic significance. The apple is described as having been picked in a garden whose master is absent; it is explicitly connected with thoughts of Eden; it is dusted like a book. A reader would have to be truly obtuse not to catch the many Biblical allusions. Indeed, the apple that appears here is not only a piece of forbidden fruit like its Biblical counterpart, it is doubly forbidden. It is so first of all in its having been plucked by a person trespassing on someone else's property. In that sense alone it is clearly a stolen apple. It is also forbidden in its having been expressly denied to someone who asks for it or at least who asks for a piece of it, its core, its remainder, the portion that is usually thrown away. Porky the tramp (who is also a pig) tells his partner who pleads for a share to "Wise up," informing him that there will be no core left. This refusal and its curt explanation give rise to all kinds of speculation.

It sounds as though the pleading tramp is asking for the core of the apple because he knows that's all he is likely to get from such a piggish person, if he is lucky enough to get anything at all. (Incidentally, it is worth noting that this seems to be the only apple available, otherwise the request by Porky's companion would make no sense.) But the core of the apple is also its center, its heart so to speak. Though it may appear near worthless to the person eating its outer flesh, the core holds the seeds that contain the potential for future growth. Porky shows no sign of thinking in such terms. He is about to consume the entire piece of fruit, core and all. Yet his refusal to share even this much of his paltry prize, selfish and uncharitable though his action may appear, can be read another way. Porky's selfishness could be interpreted as saying that when one reaches the heart of knowledge one discovers there is no core, no center that will endure and perpetuate itself. This insight may comprise the height of wisdom, which could be why Porky tells his companion to "Wise up."

Parents and teachers pass away, buildings decay, times change, even truth itself seems temporary. The permanence and stability we yearn for in our youth, the foundations of security and sustenance, turn out to be nonexistent. Is that what we learn when we wise up? Do we then stop asking for the core? Let's see how such questions fare as we move on with the poem.

The third section contains a comparison between the schools and schoolchildren of today and those of the narrator's own youth. Though he relies solely on hearsay knowledge, the narrator appears to have a low opinion of what goes on in today's schools. He feels some affinity, however, with the students who attend them. Yet, despite this connection, he suspects they would not understand his quest. The section ends with a second portrayal of the narrator's former teacher, this one somewhat grimmer than the first. Here are the lines:

I hear modern schoolchildren shine their pants
In buttock-blessing seats in steamy schools
Soaking up civics and vacant events
From innocents who sponge periodicals
And squeeze that out again in chalky gray
Across the blackboards of the modern day;

Yet they can guess why we fled our benches
Afternoons when we ourselves were just nice
Schoolkids too, who peered out through the branches
For one homely share of the centuries
—Fighting in Latin the wars of the Greeks—
Our green days, the apple we picked and picked

And that was never ours; though they would
Rake their skulls if they found out we returned
By free choice to this house of the dead,
And stand here wondering what he could have learned,
His eyes great pupils and his fishhook teeth
Sunk in the apple of knowledge or death.

The criticism of today's schools contained in the first stanza of this third section should sound familiar to most of us. The students, it is rumored, are being coddled, both mentally and physically. They sit in contoured plastic seats, rather than on hard wooden benches, in schools that are overheated, rather than drafty and cold. They study current events, rather than history and the classics, and they are taught by teachers who are themselves innocent of knowledge, and who spend their day dutifully sponging and squeezing out the useless information that their students are required to soak up. A more trenchant blast at our schools within the space of six spare lines is hard to imagine. Small wonder, agrees the sympathetic reader,

that today's students, like those of generations past, are
eager to flee as soon as the bell rings and have no trouble
guessing why their counterparts of years back wanted to
do the same.

But something's amiss with that line of reasoning.
Why should today's students want to flee school just as
badly as did those of years gone by? Haven't we just been
told that schools are more comfortable these days than
they once were and that they are less demanding in intellectual terms as well? Well, now, if today's students are
being coddled, both physically and intellectually, why are
they still dying to leave? Could it be because they *know*
they are being coddled and they somehow resent that kind
of treatment? That seems rather farfetched. Also, if the
conditions are that different between then and now, how
could today's youngsters so easily guess why students of
the past may have rushed out so hurriedly at dismissal
time that they fair knocked the door off its hinges? They
can guess, the narrator gives us to believe, because they
understand intuitively that all school children want to
leave school, no matter what classroom conditions are like
at the time. Without pausing here to consider the truth of
that generalization, let us accept it as a fact and move on
from there. For what is more interesting than the students'
desire to leave is their puzzlement over the adult who seeks
to return. Why, they ask, should anyone in his right mind
want to come back—"by free choice," no less—to this
"house of the dead"?

(For those who recall Yeats's poem, "Among School
Children," which also portrays a questioning adult in a
schoolroom setting, Kinnell's image of the schoolchildren
raking their skulls in dismay over the prospect of someone
voluntarily returning to such a grim environment will
surely call to mind Yeats's famous lines that describe how
"the children's eyes/in momentary wonder stare upon/ A
sixty-year-old smiling public man" [1973, p. 141].)

Why, indeed, the return journey? Is the narrator near-
ing an answer? It seems he might be. For the source of his

perplexity is named at last. He switches now to the first person plural, as though he had suddenly become the voice of all of his former classmates who had silently assembled at his side. *We* "stand here wondering," he says, "what he could have learned." The "he" refers of course to the speaker's former teacher.

"What he could have learned." The question is peculiarly phrased. It has a childish awkwardness, the kind of query a youngster might make who was not exactly sure of what he wanted to know. Why would someone wonder what his teacher could have learned? To explore that question we must consider once more the poem's symbolic use of the apple. Its image is brought into play twice in this section. It is first described as being picked and picked by the students without ever being possessed by them (a Sisyphean image that mirrors the frustration of the tramp's companion). We next encounter it locked firmly in the bite of what can only be the grinning skull of the former teacher, his fishhook teeth bare and protruding, his eyes now empty sockets—"great pupils," the narrator calls them. In the image of the teacher's death head tenaciously clenching the prized apple in its jaws—as though snared in a bobbing contest on Halloween—we sense echoes of Porky's selfish act in section two. However, the teacher not only refuses to give up the least remnant of his coveted possession, as did Porky, he takes the whole damned thing with him, core and all, to his grave! Small wonder that his former students must make a pilgrimage to the schoolhouse, which represents the teacher's mausoleum, to pursue their quest.

In the fourth and final section of the poem the visitor starts to recall specific lessons he was taught in his old schoolhouse. Three of them are brought to mind. The first deals with Greek literature and history, the second with what might today be called social studies, though it is actually no more than a prediction the teacher once made about the future state of things, and the third with a subject that is essentially scientific, a bit of astronomy, to be specific. All three lessons, however, are also about other matters, as we shall see. Here is the section.

> I recall a recitation in that house:
> "*We are the school of Hellas* was the claim.
> Maybe it was so. Anyway Hellas
> Thought it wasn't, and put the school to flame.
> They came back, though, and sifted the ruin."
> I think the first inkling of the lesson
>
> Was when we watched him from the apple wrest
> Something that put into him the notion
> That the earth was coming to its beautifulest
> And would be like paradise again
> As soon as he died from it. The flames went out
> In those blue mantles; he waved us to the night—
>
> And here we are, under the starlight. I
> Remember he taught us the stars disperse
> In wild flight, though constellated to the eye.
> And now I can see the night in its course,
> The slow sky uncoiling in exploding forms,
> The stars that flee it riding free in its arms.

What shall we make of these three lessons and of the way each of them is introduced? Do they bring the narrator's query to a satisfying close? Were they worth the trip, so to speak?

Well, they do help to clear up certain mysteries, or seem to—the obscurity of the statue's frozen gesture in section two, for example. If we assume the statue to have been modeled after the teacher, we now have a second reading of its fixed motion, which at first seemed to beckon yet remained obscure. This final section describes the teacher as waving his pupils to the night, shooing them away perhaps? Sending them off on their own? This wave of dismissal, we quickly realize, is also a very teacherly gesture, one that could easily be mistaken to be a beckoning call, at least from a distance in either space or time.

This ambiguity brings us to the substance of the three lessons the narrator recalled.

Each of the lessons is peculiarly convoluted. Each contains an ironic twist or change or contradiction of some kind that brings us up short, making us do a kind of double take. "We are the school of Hellas," Pericles declares. But the enemies of Athens weren't so sure that was so and they proceeded to sack the city. But what happened then? "They came back," we are told, "and sifted the ruin," just as the narrator of the poem is doing to the remnants of his former school. Do the enemies of schools always become repentant? Is that a fundamental truth of some kind? We educators would certainly wish it were so.

The teacher predicts that the earth is "coming to its beautifulest/And would be like paradise again." But then comes the kicker: "As soon as he died from it." Why must paradise await the teacher's death? That sounds like a student's fantasy rather than something the teacher himself might assert. And what of the expression "died from it"? Does that simply mean dying and going to heaven as a schoolchild might understand it? Or might it suggest dying from the pain of witnessing what happens here on earth, the way one might die from an ailment of some kind? Perhaps it means both.

The final lesson, the one about science, confronts most directly the difference between what seems to be and what is. The heavenly constellations may look permanent, the teacher explains, but they are not. The curve of the Big Dipper or the straight line of Orion's belt may appear to have been set in place by a godly geometer with a love of form, but all that is illusion. "[T]he stars disperse/In wild flight," the teacher declares. "Like students fleeing a schoolhouse," the reader silently adds.

At the close of the poem, as the narrator lifts his head skyward, in preparation for his departure, we might guess, he sees the sky and the stars in a new way, thanks in part to his teacher, who himself has fled the scene as did his former students years before. But what the narrator can now see as he looks heavenward goes far beyond science and the physical state of the universe. He now has the power to penetrate the layers of meaning that lie beneath all appearances. In short, he has gained what can only be called a poet's vision. He has demonstrated that vision in writing "The Schoolhouse." We, too, having witnessed his return and his accomplishment, may feel as though we have gained something. Teachers everywhere, even if they have never heard of Galway Kinnell, owe him a debt of thanks.

In the next chapter I shall try to draw together the themes that have been introduced so far, using as my chief object of scrutiny a first grade teacher who currently works in one of Chicago's public schools.

CHAPTER 3

"O wad some Power the giftie gie us"

Learning to See [for] Oneself in a First Grade Classroom

This chapter is about what two observers (my research assistant and I) witnessed over a period of two years in a first grade public school classroom in Chicago. Our observations yielded two different kinds of discoveries. One deals with what the children in the class were encouraged to learn about themselves, and what they may have learned about their teacher during their year as first graders. The other deals with what we ourselves learned about the process of observing in classrooms, particularly when the reason for one's being there is somewhat vague and ill-defined, as it was for us. This pair of discoveries are closely interrelated, as will soon be evident.

First, a word about the purpose of our visits and the larger investigation of which they were a part. The latter was called the Moral Life of Schools Project. Its goal was to consider the various ways in which what goes on in schools and classrooms might contribute, either positively or negatively, to the moral well-being of everyone present, principally students, of course, but not overlooking teachers and other school officials as well. In designing the project we purposely did not define what was meant by phrases like "moral life" and "moral well-being." We left those key terms undefined partly because we wanted all such definitions, if there were to be any, to emerge from our work with the teachers, who were to be our partners on the project, and partly because we were by no means sure ourselves what those terms might properly signify within the context of a school or classroom.

We naturally assumed that moral matters had chiefly to do with notions like character and virtue and, therefore, we anticipated that during our visits to classrooms we would be looking for the ways in which such desirable human qualities might be either cultivated or undermined by what went on there. Beyond that, however, we had few if any preconceptions about the form our observations would take. Thus, it is hardly an exaggeration to say that when our visits began we truly did not know what we were looking for, at least not in sufficient detail for that knowledge to serve as a guide for our observations.

Here are some rudimentary facts about the classroom we visited and its teacher, beginning with the latter. Elaine Martin, as I shall refer to her here, is a woman in her late thirties who has taught for fifteen years in public schools, mostly the first grade, having been in her current position for the past five years. She is a pleasant-looking person with auburn hair, a friendly smile, and a very engaging manner. She is married and the mother of two children.

There were twenty-eight pupils in Mrs. Martin's class during each of the two years of our visits. The class's racial composition, which also remained almost constant during that time, consisted of about equal numbers of Caucasian and African–American pupils plus four or five youngsters of Asian ancestry.

The Howe School, in which Mrs. Martin works, occupies a three-story, red brick building built in the late nineteenth century, plus a one-story extension, constructed much more recently and also of brick, housing the lower grades. The extension, in which Mrs. Martin's room is located, is separated from the main building by an asphalt-covered yard containing a jungle gym and one or two other pieces of play equipment. It is here that the younger students congregate before school and during recess.

Structurally, Mrs. Martin's classroom is rectangular and box-like. Its interior walls are made of concrete block, with windows that face an alley stretching almost the full length of one side. The floor covering is of nondescript plastic tile and the lighting fixtures, which hang on slender white rods from a ten-foot-high ceiling, are fluorescent. Across the front of the room hang blackboards; the side opposite the windows is mounted with bulletin boards that extend from waist height to about as high as an adult can reach; and the rear wall is lined with metal lockers for the pupils' coats and personal belongings. There are bookcases and a few low tables against the two side walls. One or two additional tables are located toward the rear of the room. The children's desks and chairs occupy the room's center. Mrs. Martin's desk is in the front corner next to the window. In the opposite front corner beside the blackboard and facing a small throw rug is an adult-sized chair where Mrs. Martin sits when she is conducting reading groups, an activity that occupies a large portion of each schoolday.

The furnishings of Mrs. Martin's room—the contents of the bulletin boards, the objects lying on tables and shelves, the messages on the blackboard, and so forth—are almost impossible to catalogue in full, partly because they are too numerous and also because they change from week to week and sometimes from day to day. Suffice it to say that the room, like most elementary school classrooms, offers a very stimulating visual environment. There is a lot to look at and make sense of, quite apart from the activity of the room's occupants. Some of the objects on display appear to be purely decorative, like the reproduction of an abstract painting above the front blackboard or the scalloped trim around one of the bulletin boards, but most of what one sees when casually scanning the room is of obvious instructional use, or was so at one time. There are number charts, maps, calendars, lists of various kinds, student art work, graded papers, clippings from newspapers and magazines, a cage for gerbils, a terrarium, a pencil sharpener, a computer, bottles and jars of assorted sizes, a couple of yardsticks, a few plants in varying stages of health, and much more.

As a matter of fact, Mrs. Martin's room presents more than just a visually "busy" environment in which an interested visitor might become profitably absorbed. It looks downright cluttered, almost disheveled, or at least that's the way it struck me the day I arrived to begin my observations. Several shelves were overflowing with books, many of them inserted upside down or backwards. Side tables had objects lying on top of one another. There were cardboard cartons under tables and in corners, many of which contained objects (a dusty globe of the world, for example) that looked as though they had not been used or even touched for quite some time. Moreover, the conditions I observed on that first day remained pretty much the same throughout the period of our observations. The clutter did diminish somewhat from time to time (it did so dramatically once, a day or so after I had casually said something about it to Mrs. Martin), but following each sporadic attempt to tidy things up the classroom soon returned to its customary untidiness.

The sight of this clutter was initially unsettling to me and to my assistant as well, for we didn't know what to make of it. Was it the sign of a sloppy teacher, of someone who didn't care about her work? Or did it just mean that she had other things, perhaps more important things, to worry about? After all, my own office at the university would take no prize for neatness, and yet I would not want anyone to gather from its untidy appearance that I care little about what I am doing. On the contrary, the reason my desk and adjoining surfaces are piled high with books and papers (I tell myself) is precisely because I care too much about other, more important matters to be bothered with such trivial concerns. Perhaps Mrs. Martin felt the same way. At least that was a possibility.

My spate of conjectures about this state of affairs did not end with my first visit. On subsequent days I went on to wonder what relevance, if any, this clutter might have for the project in which I was newly engaged. Was the room's untidiness of any *moral* significance? Was it sending messages to the students about the unimportance of neatness and order? Might it help to explain, for example, the messy interiors of some of their desks? Or was I just being silly to fix my attention on such a superficial matter? Should I have bothered to take note of it in the first place? What did my absorption in this aspect of the room's appearance say about *me?*

Though I had no clear idea of where such pondering was headed, I sensed during those early visits that what I was groping for went far beyond the question of what to make of the apparent disorder in Mrs. Martin's room, as significant or insignificant as that state of affairs might ultimately turn out to be. I was really asking how one should look at teachers and at classrooms when one is interested in their moral shape and substance, their moral potency one might say. I also wanted to know where I fit into the process, where my personal reactions and intuitions fit in, such as my vague feeling of uneasiness and puzzlement brought on by the room's disorderliness.

I sensed that looking for the moral significance of things, whatever that might mean, would call for a finer tuning and a closer listening to what was going on both inside and outside myself than anything I had done before. But at the same time I wasn't sure how far to trust my personal reactions to what I was witnessing. I *suspected* that this or that might be significant, but what good were suspicions? Indeed, one of my strongest suspicions of all, at least initially, was reserved for the little voice within me that kept saying, "Follow your intuitions!"

As our work on the project progressed, I did learn to listen more attentively to that inner voice of mine and so did my assistant learn to listen to his. We were aided in doing so, I believe, by our experience in Mrs. Martin's

room. We came to trust ourselves as a partial function of
our coming to trust Mrs. Martin. Or so it appeared. The
two processes certainly went hand in hand. Moreover, I
suspect (that word again!) that something like the same
thing was going on for many if not most of the twenty-
eight youngsters in the room. For they, too, grew more confident and self-assured as the year wore on. Though we
clearly cannot fully account for either set of changes—
those that took place in us or the ones that took place in
the children—we think we now understand a few of the
contributing factors, particularly as they pertain to Mrs.
Martin's role in the process. To understand even that
much, however, felt like quite an accomplishment to us
after months of what sometimes seemed like fruitless effort. Although our insights are still very tentative and
leave us a long way from cracking the code of how to look
at a school or a classroom from a moral standpoint (if indeed there is a code to crack), they are at least a step in
that direction, or so we firmly believe. In order to share
with you the basis of our conviction, while at the same
time conveying a sense of its gradual development, I must
return briefly to the sense of clutter that initiated my back-
of-the-classroom pondering.

What happened to those initial worries? They soon disappeared, I am pleased to say. The clutter stayed, mind
you, as I have already reported. What disappeared was my
concern over it. I began to overlook it as I became more
interested in other things that were going on in the room.
Ultimately I completely forgot about it, or almost so. What
actually happened, on a more emotional level, was that I
forgave Mrs. Martin for being untidy, the way one might
forgive a professor for being absentminded or a wrestler
for being ungraceful. I did so because I began to recognize
what I can only call, within the context of our project, "her
redeeming virtues."

But even that does not accurately depict the sequence
of events. What happened first was that my assistant and I
began to enjoy our visits to Mrs. Martin's room without

quite knowing why. We just liked being there. Here is an excerpt from my assistant's field notes, written on a day that began with him feeling reluctant about leaving the comfort of his study. It speaks for both of us.

> I didn't want to go to visit any classes, preferring to stay in my cloister and write, but as soon as I walked in the door of Elaine's room, I was glad I'd come. The effect was instantaneous and surprising. Standing in the hall just outside her door, I considered not going in, but one step inside and the vitality of the classroom washed over and filled me.

Here he is again, some months later, after not having visited Mrs. Martin's room for some time:

> I always leave Elaine's classroom—even now, when I haven't been there in quite a while—with a sense of pleasure and lightness. . . . I need to be aware of this sentiment and careful of how it may color my perceptions of what has gone on in Elaine's classroom.

Glad to be there. Pleasure and lightness. Instantaneous and surprising. Filled with vitality. I shared all of those reactions. How come? What caused them? I have two quick answers to those questions—one negative, the other positive, but, alas, neither satisfactory. The negative answer says that whatever it was that made Mrs. Martin's room attractive, it was nothing one can put one's finger on. The positive answer calls it "classroom climate" and lets it go at that, relying upon the widespread use of that term among educators to give it meaning. They're both right, of course, but neither answer takes us very far. What's right about them is the recognition that the moral qualities of a person or of a situation seem to float on the ether. They are part of the atmosphere. They are intuited before they

are articulated. This is why it is so vitally important to stay
in touch with one's feelings as a classroom observer. But
having tuned in sentiently to such qualities, the hard task
of articulation remains. And so it was with our shared
reaction to Mrs. Martin's room.

Once again, then, what was there about the room or
about Mrs. Martin herself that gave it or her such appeal?
My first surmise was that it had something to do with the
way she interacted with the children (and perhaps with us
as well), something about her directness and candor in
dealing with situations that others might have handled
in a more guarded or even secretive way. Here are two
examples.

After recess on days when the teacher has no supervi-
sory duty and thus has remained indoors, the children who
have been outside return to the room in various states of
readiness to resume their schoolwork. Some are excited,
others are tired, a few quite matter-of-factly take their
seats, and, almost invariably, one or two have stories to tell
the teacher, sometimes tearfully, about what happened
on the playground. Many of the stories are about injustice
and cruelty. They often include accusations. Martha
yanked Sarah's ball away. Freddy pushed Billy and then
kicked him when he was down. An unknown assailant hit
Inez from behind as she was hanging from the jungle gym.
And so it goes, one calamity after another. It is not always
clear what the children expect Mrs. Martin to do about
their tales of woe. Sometimes all they seem to want is sympathy, but at other times they are obviously seeking re-
venge of some kind, which they expect Mrs. Martin to dis-
pense—in the form of a punishment or a scolding perhaps.

Mrs. Martin always takes these incidents seriously, but
seldom deals with them privately. Even when she bends
down to comfort a crying child, she rarely speaks in sub-
dued tones. Instead, she discusses what happened in a
voice that conveys sympathy and concern, and also usually can be heard several feet away, often across the room.
As a result, what might have been treated as a tête-à-tête

becomes instead a semipublic exchange that can be readily witnessed and listened to by all.

The openness with which these conversations are conducted has a strange effect. Instead of piquing the curiosity of the other students, and making them rush over to learn more about what happened, as one might think would occur, Mrs. Martin's matter-of-fact handling of the situation seems to have a calming effect. Because they can easily hear what is being said without standing right next to Mrs. Martin and the child who is doing the complaining, most of the pupils remain in their seats or go about their business as usual, putting coats away, taking out books, sharpening pencils, and so forth. There is an obvious attentiveness on the part of many to what is being said, but few pupils seem morbidly curious about the incident.

In addition to expressing the teacher's concern, something else seems to me to be conveyed to the class as a whole by the way these brief exchanges are conducted. Their semipublic nature announces to one and all that there are few secrets in this room, few subjects that cannot be talked about openly and loudly enough for everyone to hear. No need to go whispering behind people's backs, accusing them of this or that. Have a complaint? Then speak up and have it dealt with out in the open, the way one might discuss a difficulty one was having in arithmetic or reading. The voice of solace and the voice of instruction are practically indistinguishable.

Here is another example of a similar phenomenon. It comes from my assistant's notes. The situation it remarks upon is this: Once or twice a week Mrs. Evans, a volunteer who is also a retiree, comes to the room to help the children with their spelling. She works with a small group of children at a low table in the back of the room while Mrs. Martin works with reading groups in the front corner beside the chalkboard. On this particular day the children working with Mrs. Evans were a bit too loud for both women. This triggered a conversation that my assistant reports as follows:

Mrs. Evans said "I don't like this. I don't like when children are just playing." She was speaking to Elaine (Mrs. Martin) apparently. Elaine then replied to the effect that Mrs. Evans could send the kids to their seats if they weren't behaving or doing what they should be doing. "I'm very happy to help them," Mrs. Evans went on, "but they have to be working." The content of the conversation was less interesting than the nature of it. It was two women talking to one another across the room and acting as if they were [sitting side by side]. They were talking to one another when it seems pretty clear that what they really wanted to do was to talk to the kids. They were communicating a message to the kids [at Mrs. Evans's table], but they were speaking to one another, in a sense allowing the kids to overhear their thoughts and perhaps . . . draw their own conclusions.

The phrase, "allowing the kids to overhear their thoughts," certainly epitomizes what was going on in that situation, but I read it as doing more than that. To me it brings to mind the work of a magician or some other person with magical powers, like a teacher as seen by a first-grader, perhaps. After all, thoughts cannot be overheard except as they are spoken aloud and then they are no longer merely thoughts. Or are they? What is the difference between what we think and what we say? Is there one? Need there be?

I doubt that the children's thoughts were actually pulled in those directions as they overheard the two women speaking, but it wouldn't surprise me to find them thinking of matters that went far beyond the content of the conversation itself. For I am convinced that beneath the seemingly innocent banter between Mrs. Evans and Mrs. Martin lurk issues of deeper significance, as they did beneath the conversations that took place after recess. Here, as there, one of the things being tampered with—tem-

porarily erased, one might say—is the line between the
public and the private, between what is meant to be heard
by everyone and what one might confide to one's companion. What is the point of that erasure? Is it just a pedagog-
ical gimmick, a sly way of getting across a warning that
might otherwise be ignored? That is one way of reading it,
certainly. Indeed, that may be all the two women were
seeking to accomplish at the time. Nonetheless, I cannot
help thinking that more was being accomplished than
that, although not necessarily intentionally, and perhaps
without anyone's conscious awareness.

In the first place I suspect that minuscule events such
as this one contribute, albeit infinitesimally, to the quality
of openness and candor that my assistant and I found so
appealing. What is being transmitted in this brief exchange is a variation of the implicit message commented
upon earlier, which is that this is a room in which one need
harbor few secrets, in which the channels of communica-
tion are usually open and the volume of speech, at least
when what is being talked about bears on matters of conduct, is loud enough for all to hear. But there is more going
on here than that. Semipublic exchanges such as these invite all who witness them to draw a variety of conclusions
about the speakers, and about the relationship between
what is being said and one's own opinions and personal
judgments. In short, they encourage listeners *to place
themselves* in relation to the content of the conversation
and, if necessary, to take sides with respect to what is being
said. When such brief invitations to form judgments are
offered repeatedly over an extended period of time our relationship with the speakers begins to crystallize. We find
ourselves beginning to like this person and dislike that
one, to trust one and distrust the other, and so forth. We
also begin to see ourselves as occupying a position vis-à-
vis those we like or dislike, trust or distrust. We not only
like them; we *agree* with them. We not only *trust* them; we
seek them out in time of need. All of this can be summarized
by saying that we get to know people and often have strong

opinions about them after we have been around them for a while. Nothing unusual about that, to be sure. However, there are two observations to make about that common-place, each of which has special relevance to what we observed going on in Mrs. Martin's room.

One is that those relationships between ourselves and our surroundings that develop incrementally and without much conscious awareness, as many do, often leave us at a loss to explain why we feel or think as we do. We wind up liking or disliking a person, a place, or a thing, yet we are hard pressed to say why. The absence of clear-cut explanations for these attachments and aversions has special significance for teachers of young children for it is during those early years, as we know, that so many fundamental likes and dislikes (liking to read, for example, or liking school in general) are established. Yet it is precisely then that the power to ascribe cause, whether real or fanciful, is minimal. Thus, we should not be surprised to find, as we typically do, that children are unable to tell us much about *why* they like or dislike this or that about school and that the explanations they do give—"She's mean" "He's nice" "It's hard" "It's fun"—are too abbreviated to yield much insight. What this means, I believe, is that those of us who study schools and classrooms need to develop a special sensitivity to the relatively benign forces, the educational equivalents of wind and rain, that doubtless contribute to the slow weathering of the pupil's psyche.

The second observation to make about this common-place process, by which we come to a deepened understanding of ourselves and others, is that some kinds of experiences prompt us to be more exploratory and adventuresome in this regard than do others. This fact became increasingly evident to us as observers as we began to see the conversations that my assistant and I have described take on new significance as part of a larger pattern of interactions whose potential impact on the students in the class seemed to us worthy of note. This pattern did not jump out at us at once. In fact, we did not begin to notice it until we had visited the classroom many times, and come to know not only the routines of the day but the idiosyncracies of many of the students. That process of acclimatization took several months, which is worth noting because of what it implies about conducting the kind of research we were doing. Perhaps others would have seen what we saw and understood its significance far more quickly than we did, but, if so, I would have to call them lucky rather than keener than we as observers. For I know of no shortcuts that reveal in a flash the potential significance of the ordinary and humdrum aspects of classroom life. Indeed, I'm not even sure that I yet fully grasp the meaning of what I am about to describe.

Mrs. Martin does something a bit out of the ordinary when she observes pupils who are either blatantly violating, or whom she *suspects* of violating, one of the many rules that govern the conduct of the class—an occurrence, by the way, that is by no means unusual in a roomful of first graders, as one might well imagine. Instead of confronting the wrongdoer with the fact or the suspicion of his or her wrongdoing, and then proceeding to scold or admonish as circumstances warrant, she usually invites the youngster to consider his or her own actions and to categorize them in some way, to give them definition. These brief conversations frequently take place when Mrs. Martin is seated at the front of the room, working with one of the reading groups, and the offender, real or suspected, is at his or her desk or at one of the back tables. Thus, like the dialogues that take place after recess, or the across-the-room exchange between Mrs. Evans and Mrs. Martin that I just described, these exchanges are commonly conducted in a tone of voice that allows the whole class to listen in. Here is one such conversation, for which I must first provide a context.

In arithmetic the pupils were being taught to combine coins of different value to produce a given amount. They were shown, for example, that the sum of seventeen cents could be made up of seventeen pennies or a dime and seven pennies or three nickels and two pennies, and so forth. Once the procedure had been explained to the class as a whole, and was seemingly understood by everyone, the children were instructed to work in pairs to demonstrate their mastery of the principle. This was to be done in the following way. On one of the back tables were placed a set of four rubber stamps, an ink pad, and a small box containing white slips of paper. The four stamps displayed the faces of a penny, a nickel, a dime, and a quarter. On the front blackboard was a list of numbers representing amounts of money, all less than a dollar. The assignment called for using the stamps to depict an appropriate combination of coins equal to each of the assigned amounts, one solution per slip of paper, which the teacher would later inspect for accuracy. Each child was to work with a partner who was to share the task of deciding what combination of coins to use and also take turns using the stamps. The children were allowed to work on the assignment whenever they were not engaged in formal instruction, provided that no one else was at the table at the time and that they could find a partner to work with.

On this particular morning Calvin, who is a bit of a cutup, is at the table alone, fiddling with the rubber stamps. Mrs. Martin, who is seated at the front of the room with one of her reading groups, looks up and sees him.

"Calvin?" she says.

"Yes?" replies Calvin.

"What are you doing?"

"Uh, I'm working with the stamps."

"Who are you supposed to have with you, Calvin?"

"Huh?"

"Who are you supposed to have with you?"

"Uh, my partner."

"Do you have a partner, Calvin?"

Calvin slowly turns his head to his left and then, just as slowly, to his right, as though he were looking to see whether there might be someone standing beside him.

"No," he says.

"What should you do, Calvin?" Mrs. Martin asks.

Calvin does not reply. He returns to his desk and sits down. Mrs. Martin turns back to her reading group.

Here is another instance of something similar, this one comes from my assistant's field notes: Mrs. Martin is working with a reading group when she notices that Kevin and Judith, who are seated side by side at their desks, are talking with one another.

"Kevin and Judith, are you visiting or helping?" she asks.

"I'm working," says Kevin.

"Visiting," says Judith.

Mrs. Martin pauses for an instant, then asks, "Kevin, do you think you can sit there and work quietly without talking to yourself or to Judith?"

"I think so," says Kevin.

She then asks exactly the same question of Judith, who says she thinks she needs to move. Mrs. Martin sends her to an empty desk on the opposite side of the room. Several minutes later Mrs. Martin notices the two of them together again at Kevin's desk and once again asks if they are visiting or helping.

"Helping," they both chorus.

I cannot resist offering one more example just to add variety to what has already been presented. In this instance Mrs. Martin, again with a reading group, observes Michael, who is wandering around the teacher's desk, looking at this and that.

"What are you looking for, Michael?" she asks.

"Nothing," Michael replies.

"Oh," Mrs. Martin says, "I thought you were." She continues to look at him for a second or two as he quietly returns to his seat.

These brief interrogations, many of them carried on with the two speakers yards apart, occurred so frequently in Mrs. Martin's classroom that beyond growing accustomed to their occurrence, we ultimately came to think of them as Mrs. Martin's special way of dealing with the minor disruptions that every teacher of young children must face. But our thoughts about them went deeper than that. For we both sensed that the way Mrs. Martin dealt with such matters had something to do with what we liked

about visiting her room. We also suspected (by now a
friendly word) that this characteristic of Mrs. Martin's
style might bear upon what the children there were being
given the opportunity to learn about themselves and about
how people get along together.

From the standpoint of the pupils, what is common to
all of these episodes is that the children being questioned
are invited by the teacher to step outside their own skin, to
see their actions from an external perspective and often to
give them a name or label from that perspective. The invitation may take the form of a fairly neutral query, as when
the children are simply asked, "What are you doing?" or it
may provide them with options to use in their description,
as when Mrs. Martin asks, "Are you visiting or helping?"
Occasionally Mrs. Martin offers her own perspective,
which reveals to the children how their actions are actually seen by someone else, as when she says, "I thought you
were [looking for something]."

Being questioned in this way encourages the children
to become judges of their own actions. Yet the freedom
to make those judgments, as the process also makes clear,
is by no means unconstrained. The categories by which to
judge are often set in advance and are usually few in number. There are other people present who are doing the judging as well—the teacher, one's classmates who are looking
on, and sometimes an adult observer or two—which
means that one's own judgment may not only be tested
against those of others but may sometimes be contested,
called into question, disagreed with. The public nature of
the process, the fact that the children are asked not only to
judge, but also to *announce* their judgments in a voice that
all can hear, not only opens the door to falsifying one's response, it also entails an act of commitment, a form of giving one's word. In short, it calls upon the children to see
themselves, if not as others see them, then at least as they
choose in that particular circumstance to be seen by
others.

What might such a process do to those who observe
it—the student onlookers and the adult visitors? Obvi-

ously, I can't speak for the students, but it's hard to imagine them witnessing those little exchanges day after day without it having some effect on them. Did they sense in Mrs. Martin's questions the kind of respect for their point of view that I, as an observer, sensed was there? Again, I can't say that they did, but the seriousness of the pupils' demeanor in responding certainly indicated that they took Mrs. Martin's queries seriously, which may be all we will ever know about the actual impact of such exchanges.

And what about the two observers? What did those episodes do to us? Speaking for the pair of us, I can certainly say they started us thinking along lines that proved to be fruitful. As for myself, what impressed me most at the time and what continues to do so now, these several months later, is the multifaceted nature of each of the situations I have described, plus the scores of other situations that my assistant and I noted but that I have not commented upon here. Each of them, when held up to scrutiny, takes on a depth of psychological significance whose intricacy is sometimes close to breathtaking. In this respect they are like pebbles brought back from the beach, the kind that when dipped in water reveal colors and layered complexities that arrest the eye and stir the imagination. But these classroom events differ from pebbles in that *their* complexities always include moral dimensions of one kind or another, or so it seemed to me.

Consider the little moral drama encased in the brief interchange between Kevin, Judith, and Mrs. Martin. Kevin said he was working, while Judith described herself as visiting. Kevin said he thought he could work quietly in the future, whereas Judith acknowledged that the temptation to talk would be too great for her and, therefore, she requested a move. A few minutes later, when they were seen back at Kevin's desk, they both readily agreed that they were helping each other.

Is it fruitful to think about what was going on there from the standpoint of lying versus telling the truth? I'm not sure. It is tempting to conclude that Kevin was lying at the start and Judith telling the truth, but what about their joint response to the final query? Was Judith now lying, along with Kevin, or was Kevin now telling the truth, along with Judith? Whichever it was, Mrs. Martin did not seem to care. She did not challenge the pair's final declaration. She took them at their word. Was that because she had come to the same judgment herself and therefore agreed with them, or was it for some other reason? Did she perhaps think that the act of declaring themselves to be helping each other would suffice to bring such a condition into being even if it was not there to start with? Or did she have something else on her mind? What else *could* she have been thinking of?

Turning to the episode involving Calvin and the rubber stamps, what shall we make of his looking methodically from side to side when Mrs. Martin asks him if he has a partner? From Mrs. Martin's point of view the question was surely rhetorical. Obviously, she could see that Calvin had no partner. Yet he responded to the question nonrhetorically. He treated it as though it were a genuine request for information. Or did he? Did he really think for an instant that he might have had a partner beside him whom he had somehow overlooked? Surely not. But why, then, the turning of the head? Was it because he did not yet understand the significance of a rhetorical question? Might he have been aware that the eyes of other students (and one other adult) were upon him at that instant and have chosen this way of responding in order to save face, or perhaps in the hope of drawing a laugh from his classmates? Come to think of it, why did Mrs. Martin ask the question that way in the first place? Does asking questions like that just come naturally to Mrs. Martin? Is it enough to say that she is just that kind of person, or does she have to think about them, or might she have had to do so at one time?

Even the exchange involving Michael, brief as it was, contained its share of mystery, also with moral overtones. What *was* Michael doing at his teacher's desk? Mrs. Martin thought he was looking for something. But was he? Or might he have just been idly exploring? And was that what Mrs. Martin really thought, or did she suspect him of doing more than just looking?

One of the interesting things about this kind of pondering is that once begun there seems to be no stopping it. And it is not just that the particular events on which one has focused seem endlessly fascinating and worthy of contemplation. It is rather that one begins to wonder if *everything* that goes on in classrooms, or the world for that matter, might take on that kind of complexity if one were to give it time, take it seriously. To return to the beachcomber's analogy, maybe all pebbles are worth saving if one looks closely enough. That is certainly what the Romantics declared at the close of the eighteenth century. It is what Wordsworth intimates when he says, "To me the meanest flower that blows can give/ Thoughts that do often lie too deep for tears" (1983, p. 555). It is also what Blake talks about when he speaks of seeing "a World in a Grain of Sand,/ And a Heaven in a Wild Flower" (1927, p. 118).

But that Romantic insight, at least when taken to its extreme, is of limited help to today's classroom observer who, figuratively speaking, cannot begin to cleanse and admire every pebble on the beach. Given that obvious limitation, the question becomes: what to pause and reflect upon from among all the sights and sounds that one witnesses? It is at this point that I begin to fall back on what I said earlier about the importance of hunches, suspicions, intuitions, and the like. In a nutshell, the rule of thumb seems to be: Consider what interests you. Follow you nose. But acting on that advice requires a kind of trust and confidence in oneself that is not easily attained or maintained. Moreover, how does one avoid error when following one's nose?

The trivial answer, of course, is that one doesn't. Getting lost from time to time is an inevitable part of the process, and part of the fun as well, when conditions are right. A more serious answer, however, would address the education of our sensibilities, how we learn to hone our perceptual apparatus, and how we transform what we know and read into daily habits of looking and listening. Obviously, there is a lot more to be said about this process. I leave what little I know of it for future writings and close this chapter with the following fantasy:

I am sitting in the back of Mrs. Martin's classroom on a lovely spring morning when she looks up and sees me staring out the window at the freshly budding trees. "What are you doing, Philip," she asks, "are you visiting or working?" "I'm doing both, teacher," I reply with serious demeanor, though privately I am a bit chagrined that my inattentiveness is apparent, "And I'm doing much more besides," I add under my breath, "I'm also learning *how* to visit and *how* to work. Like so many of your students, I'm still trying to figure out how to see for myself, believe it or not. Things are coming on though, Mrs. Martin, they're coming on." At that point I break into a smile. Mrs. Martin smiles back, without comment of course. Her reading group, all five members of which have been listening to our exchange, patiently awaits her renewed attention.

CHAPTER 4

What Teaching Does to Teachers

A Personal Tale

Initially I had intended to include in this book only the material contained in the preceding three chapters. With minor changes, those chapters comprise the Julius and Rosa Sachs Memorial Lectures, which I delivered at Teachers College in the fall of 1990. However, even before those lectures were fully written I began to think of adding a fourth to round out the set of perspectives the three lectures covered. The first lecture was to treat one of my former teachers; the second one, a teacher portrayed in a work of art—a poem; and the third, a teacher whom I had recently observed in action. All three were designed to explore the enduring, though often unrecognized effects, that teachers sometimes have on their students. What was missing, I realized, was a look at the effects of teaching from the opposite direction, from the perspective of a teacher himself or herself, for whom the relevant question would be: How has my own teaching affected me?

For such a view to be as probing as possible it should be solely autobiographical, I thought, rather than only partially so. In other words, instead of interviewing one or more teachers to find out what they thought about the effect of their own work on themselves, a better plan, or so it seemed, would be to take a close look at myself as a teacher and at what teaching had done to me. Interviewing myself would allow me to follow my thoughts wherever they might lead, without fear of reticence or embarrassment or any of the other shortcomings that threaten the veracity of ordinary interviews. I vowed to do just that as soon as possible, although I knew it would not be in time to include whatever I came up with as part of the already-announced series of lectures.

When I finally got around to acting on that intention what actually emerged from my ruminations was quite different from what I had anticipated. I did wind up thinking about teaching from a different perspective than the ones employed in the preceding three chapters. That much went according to plan. Moreover, my thoughts at least began by dutifully reflecting on my own teaching and how it may have affected my life. However, before very long my reflections began to stray rather far afield from the prescribed topic. Rather than trying to pull them back, I let them go where they would, hoping that the path they took would ultimately lead home. It did so, thankfully, and as often happens in such situations the circuitous route my thoughts took proved to be instructive in its own right. Consequently, I have retained most of my meanderings in this report of where my thoughts led. I hope that others too may find the route taken worth the time required to retrace it with me.

*   *   *

The main reason for my initially veering from the path of trying to figure out how a life of teaching may have made me a different person than I otherwise might have been was that I found I couldn't answer the question satisfactorily. About the only thing I could say for certain concerning the impact of teaching on my life was that I possess many memories that I surely would not have were it not for the fact that I have been a teacher. I can recall scenes, events, and episodes from my teaching experience much as I remember images from vacations I have taken or countries I have visited. I also remember the names and can picture the faces of many of my former students and colleagues. Like everyone else, I possess a kind of internal photograph album that I can flip through at leisure, conjuring up before my mind's eye a dim yet distinct image of this or that person from my teaching past. The bulk of its pages are blank, to be sure, and even the names beneath most of the missing pictures are illegible. But enough of it remains to serve as demonstrable evidence, at least to myself, that I have indeed been a teacher for many years.

So if I restrict my search to the contents of my memory, I have no difficulty whatsoever in gathering hard evidence of how teaching has changed me. But memories of past experience, as delightful as they may be to savor from time to time (or as painful, which they can also be) were not exactly what I had in mind when I first began to think about my personal indebtedness to teaching. What I was looking for was something a little more integral to my life than are memories per se, something like a set of character traits, perhaps, or personality characteristics, or even an idiosyncrasy or two.

From thoughts about the many memories of teaching that I have piled up over the years, I was next led to consider how my characteristic ways of teaching have changed during that time. There, too, is something I can speak of with certainty. Moreover, the process of thinking about how my teaching had changed over time seemed to draw me closer to the goal of understanding how teaching has affected me.

A couple of items came readily to mind. There is no doubt, I quickly realized, that I lecture less today than in years past, and instead spend more time leading discussions. Further, I have changed the content of what I teach, a change that goes along with the altered instructional format. I now prefer to concentrate on a small number of texts, reading and discussing each one carefully, rather than trying to cover as much material as possible, which I used to do when lecturing. But once again, given the goal of trying to figure out how teaching has changed me, those alternations in teaching style and content still seemed off the mark.

At first, I wasn't sure why that was so. After all, I reasoned, if the way I behave in class has changed, must not *I* have changed as well? It would seem so, but maybe not. Mightn't it be possible for one to modify one's technique as a teacher without at the same time altering the enduring qualities that comprise one's psychological makeup? Where, in other words, does the "I" stop and the teacher with his favored ways of handling the demands of teaching begin?

As I thought about that last question it occurred to me that changes such as the two I have mentioned—the shift from lecture to discussion methods and my recent preference for the close reading of a few texts—reflected a number of less visible and perhaps deeper changes that I have undergone over the years, changes having to do with my view of life in general, and of teaching in particular. As an instance of the latter, I no longer feel the same compulsion I once felt to learn as much as I can about all that is going on my field. That is so in part, I believe, because teaching is no longer epitomized for me by the image of an extremely knowledgeable person passing on neatly packaged bundles of what he or she knows to someone else. That standard view of teaching reasserts itself from time to time, I must confess, so as an ideal it has by no means disappeared completely. But within the order of my own system of beliefs it no longer enjoys the commanding position it once had.

There remain problems, however, with accepting that kind of testimony as evidence of how teaching has changed me. For even if I could show that my outlook on teaching has undergone important changes over the years and that such change is tied to even more general shifts in my view of the world, I am left to ask whether those transformations have grown out of my experience as a teacher or have been caused by something else. Another way to frame the question is to ask which has happened: Has my teaching changed *me* or have I changed my teaching? Most likely, both have occurred. But unless one can differentiate between the two—between oneself, pure and simple, and oneself as a teacher, as the occupant of an occupational role—how is it possible to talk about what teaching does to teachers? In the light of that seeming impossibility, I thought to myself, maybe the thing to do would be to abandon the project.

As my thoughts limped along in this desultory way, I recalled a series of studies I had undertaken with a couple of colleagues very near the beginning of my academic career, more than thirty years ago. We were interested in finding out how the personality of teachers changed over time. In pursuit of that interest we had administered a paper-and-pencil test, The Edwards Personal Preference Schedule, to scores of teachers and teachers-in-training around the country. The Edwards PPS, as the test was referred to by those who worked with it, yielded scores on a dozen or more psychological "needs" that were presumed to underlie the test-taker's preference for one kind of activity over another. Thus, a person who consistently selected items describing activities that involved being deferent to others, such as writing thank you notes or being a porter, would achieve a score that marked him or her as having a high "need" to express deference. One who preferred activities of a nurturing kind, such as preparing meals for the elderly or taking care of a pet, would score high on the need to be nurturing. And so on.

What the findings revealed about teachers as a group was that they scored above average in deference, nurture, and endurance and below average in what the test referred to as "heterosexual interests." Moreover (and this was the important point), when we grouped the teachers according to their years of teaching experience that same profile of needs with its three peaks and one valley—high scores on *deference, nurture* and *endurance* and a low score on *heterosexuality*—became more pronounced with each successive decade of experience. What it looked like, in other words, was either that teaching actually *produced* that particular combination of needs, that this was how teach-

ing affected teachers, or that teachers who lacked the
requisite profile of characteristics were gradually weeded
out of the profession, leaving behind a group whose members began to look more and more alike in each successive
cohort when arranged by years of experience. Of course,
both of these possibilities could be in operation at the
same time, which is to say, both a formative and a selective
influence could have been at work at once.

Why this particular set of needs? That seemed easy
enough to explain after the fact, though none of us had pre-
dicted the pattern we discovered. The high need to be nurturing made perfect sense, we thought. After all, a teacher's job is to nurture the young. We further reasoned that
the work teachers do is often trying, which might explain
their apparent preference for activies that called for endurance. Their need to be mild mannered and subservient
to authorities, such as the building principal and central
office administrators, would account for their scoring high
on the need to be deferent, or so we imagined. We had no
easy explanation for the lowered scores in the domain of
heterosexual activities—"Lo het" was the way it was abbreviated in our statistical summaries—but we reasoned
that teaching had long been a profession that had at-
tracted more than its share of single men and women and
that the teacher's social isolation, his or her lack of adult
companionship during most of the working day, might actually serve to diminish an already reduced level of heterosexual interests within the group as a whole. All of this
was pure conjecture of course, but it sounded reasonable
to us at the time.

In any case, the overall profile of scores was striking
enough to make us believe that we had unearthed a set of
characteristics distinctive of teachers in general and perhaps produced or at least accentuated by the conditions
under which teachers typically work. Needless to say, we
were excited by what we thought was a discovery of some
importance to educators. We were so pleased, in fact, we
even became a bit giddy and joked about our results. A

popular song at that time had lyrics that began, "You load sixteen tons and wha da ya get? Another day older and deeper in debt." We adapted the words to our findings and would amuse each other from time to time by singing: "You teach sixteen years and wha da ya get? A little more deferent and lower in het."

Our excitement and the humor it spawned did not last long. We had known when we began our investigation that the version of the Edwards PPS we were using had been standardized on a college population, a practice that was and probably still is fairly common among test developers. A more extensive set of norms, which would include older subjects, had been promised by the test publisher and did indeed appear shortly after we had completed the first analysis of our data. We naturally suspected that some of the differences we had observed would turn out to be age-related, but we were quite unprepared for how completely that was so. The new norms washed away almost all of our findings. Except for being rather more deferent than average in their early twenties, a fact that was hardly more than puzzling when considered by itself, teachers looked no different than anyone else of corresponding age. So much for our discovery.

Looking back on that experience today, I suspect that if we had persevered, and if we had had more sophisticated statistical techniques at our disposal, we might have teased out an occupationally specific pattern of needs and possibly even one that grew more distinct in each succeeding age group of teachers. However, the new norms made clear that within our sample, age-related characteristics were much more powerfully evident than were any belonging to teachers as professionals, so we abandoned the project and moved on to other things. How teaching might affect teachers we left for others to explore.

What makes the account of that experience pertinent here is not just the obvious similarity between the question my colleagues and I were asking those many years ago and the one I began exploring in connection with the writ-

ing of this chapter. The parallel between the two situations
goes beyond that. In addition to the questions being alike,
there is also a striking similarity in what happened while
pursuing them. In both instances the decision to abandon
the project, or at least the thought of doing so, arose
quickly, almost as soon as the discouraging news of there
being no quick discoveries to be made began to be evident.

In the first case we well might have continued to explore the question of how teaching affects teachers simply
by shifting to some other psychological test or, better yet,
by employing a whole battery of tests. The cost of doing so
would not have been trivial in either time or energy, but
neither would it have been prohibitive. In the present situation I could easily prolong my Proustian search for the
marks teaching has left on me. The only cost to me would
be the time spent in doing so. In both instances, however,
the prospect of going on was unappealing.

Why was this so? Why this reluctance to continue? Is
it just a matter of being easily discouraged or is there more
to it than that? To find out what the trouble might be requires taking a closer look at the initial question: *How
does teaching affect teachers?*

That certainly sounds like a reasonable question to in-
vestigate, and even an important one. A lot seems to hang
on its answer. Consider, for example, what might follow
from the discovery that teaching had a consistently negative effect on its practitioners, that it wore them down, let's
say, or "burned them out," as we hear of it doing these days.
Surely knowledge of that kind would be of considerable
use in determining how to rectify the situation. Or imagine this. Imagine my being able to testify with absolute
certainty that a near lifetime of teaching had made me a
better person in some clearly definable way (or a worse
one, for that matter!). Mightn't such testimony, especially
if echoed by other teachers, be of use to teacher educators
and to others as well, including whoever is in charge of
recruiting newcomers to the profession? Think, for example, what it would mean if we could assure those newcomers that they stood a very strong chance of continuing

to grow in wisdom and contentment as they matured in their chosen profession. Wouldn't such knowledge be worth whatever time and effort it might take to uncover it? Surely the answer has to be yes.

Why, then, give up the search just because of a few early setbacks? One possibility, the one intimated by both of the experiences I have reported, is that there is no answer to the question, that a lifetime of teaching leaves no discernible marks on anyone or at least none worth ferreting out and talking about. There are two sound reasons to reject that possibility. One is that it contradicts popular opinion. The other is that it makes no sense to me personally. Each of these reasons deserves comment.

Popular opinion has it that what we do for a living does indeed make a difference in the kind of persons we turn out to be. It is this belief that accounts for the prevalence of occupational stereotypes in books and movies and elsewhere. Lawyers are portrayed as being avaricious, policemen as tough, clergymen as mild mannered, and so forth. Their jobs demand it of them, and thus help to make them that way, or so we believe. Teachers as a group have by no means escaped this kind of stereotyping. As a matter of fact, it was just such a stereotyped portrayal that got us interested in seeing how teachers would respond to the Edwards Personal Preference Schedule.

One of the influences that triggered our research was the picture of teachers presented in Willard Waller's book, *The Sociology of Teaching*, which was written in 1932 and had become a classic by the time we began our investigation some twenty-five years or so later. Part Five of that book, a section entitled "What Teaching Does to Teachers," opens with a spate of assertions about the formative effect of being a teacher. "Teaching makes the teacher," Waller (1932) writes,

> Teaching is a boomerang that never fails to come back to the hand that threw it. . . . [I]ts most pronounced effect is upon the teacher. Teaching does something to those who teach. Introspective teachers know of

changes that have taken place in themselves. Objectively minded persons have observed the relentless march of growing teacherishness in others. (p. 375)

With that as an introduction, Waller goes on to document what that "relentless march of teacherishness" does to people. He precedes his description with the observation that most people who have commented on what teachers are like have done so in an unfriendly manner. Here is what that unfriendly portrait of teachers includes:

There is first that certain inflexibility or unbendingness of personality which is thought to mark the person who has taught. That stiff and formal manner into which the young teacher compresses himself every morning . . . becomes, they say, a plaster cast which at length he cannot loosen. One has noticed, too, that in his personal relationships the teacher is marked by reserve, an incomplete personal participation in the dynamic social situation and a lack of spontaneity, . . . As if this reserve were not in itself enough, . . . it is supplemented . . . by certain outward barriers which prevent all and sundry from coming into contact with the man behind the mask. . . . Along with this goes dignity, . . . which is not natural dignity like that of the American Indian, but . . . [a kind] that consists of an abnormal concern over a restricted role and the restricted but well defined status that goes with it. . . . The didactic manner, the authoritative manner, the flat, assured tones of voice that go with them, are bred in the teacher by his dealings in the school room, where he rules over the petty concerns of children as a Jehovah none too sure of himself. . . . It is said, and it would be difficult to deny it, that the teacher mind is not creative. . . . There are other traits which some observers have mentioned: a set of the lips, a look of strain, a certain kind of smile, a studied mediocrity, a glib mastery of platitude. Some observers have remarked that a certain way of standing about, the way of a person who has had to spend much of his time waiting for something to happen and has had to be very dignified about it, is characteristic of the teacher. . . . Henry Adams has said that no man can be a school master for ten years and remain fit for anything else, and his statement has given many a teacher something to worry about. (pp. 381–82)

Following this depressing portrayal of what teachers in the early 1930s looked like to the "unfriendly observer," Waller announces that there is also a positive side to the picture, which he proceeds to sketch. "Teaching brings out pleasant qualities in some persons," he says, "and for them it is the most gratifying vocation in the world." Among the pleasant qualities that teaching is said to breed in some teachers, according to Waller, are "patience and fairness and a reserve that is only gentlemanly and never frosty" (p. 383). There are some persons, he concludes, "whom teaching liberates, and these sense during their first few months of teaching a rapid growth and expansion of personality" (p. 383).

These more cheerful comments, which represent the views of *friendly* observers, presumably, as opposed to unfriendly ones, do balance the picture somewhat. But the overall impression remains a gloomy one. Moreover, the gloom does not go away when Waller turns to the more detailed question of how teachers get to be the way they are. Here he is discussing the effect of shop talk among teachers:

Many younger teachers, when they are thrown into a group of teachers who live teaching, breathe teaching, dream teaching, and have teaching as a garnish for every meal, undergo a personal degeneration sometimes called "the reduction of personality." The reduction of personality results from the transition from a wide and stimulating range of contacts to a much narrower attentional field; a loss of faith in subtler and less easily accessible personal satisfaction, a regression toward the elemental, an inner grief and longing for the things that were, covered by an outward cynicism of the

most callous and brutal sort; . . . The reduction of personality occurs among teachers when they leave the
brilliant world of college for the more prosaic world in
which they are to teach. . . . This is what sets the ultimate limit to the amount of shop-talk in which teachers
can indulge without incurring those vicious tissue-
changes that go with overindulgence. (pp. 431–432)

Waller went on to report that these "vicious tissue
changes," which comprise "the adaptation of personality
to teaching" occurred rapidly, typically "within the first
few weeks of teaching experience" (p. 433).

This discussion of Waller's views has traveled a circuitous route. It began as an effort to reject the suggestion
that our abandonment of the how-teaching-affects-
teachers question back in the 1950s was based on there re-
maining little hope of our ever finding anything once our
initial efforts came to naught. The prevalence and durabil-
ity of occupational stereotypes, which include depictions
of teachers, should be sufficient, I argued, to keep that
hope alive for a considerable length of time despite minor
setbacks. However, having now reported in some detail on
the substance of the teacher stereotype as portrayed in
Waller's book, a portrayal that actually spurred us on in
our work, I have come to sense things that I seem to have
overlooked or was insufficiently aware of back then.

First of all, the depth, if not to say the viciousness, of
Waller's prejudice toward teachers jumps out at me now
with a starkness that was lacking thirty years ago. I realized of course, even back then, that the view he presented
was rather extreme. But I discounted the significance of
that fact on two grounds. First, I reasoned that Waller's
portrait of teachers was out-of-date. After all, the book was
already twenty five years old when I first came upon it. Its
datedness, I believed, largely accounted for some of the
negative things that were said—the emphasis placed
on the teacher's prudishness, for example. Moreover, the
fact that Waller almost always spoke of the teacher as "he"

and that he mentioned such obvious anachronisms as the teacher "putting on his collar" in the morning, clearly reinforced the impression of the book being very out-of-date in certain respects.

Second, I accepted (all too readily, I now realize) Waller's gestures in the direction of being fair and objective. After all, the views he presented were the opinions of "unfriendly observers" and not the author's own, as he took care to point out. Moreover, he sought to present both sides of the picture, as we would expect a fair-minded and objective person (a professor, no less!) to do. Teachers are seen as mediocre and uncreative by some observers. Waller wanted his readers to understand, but they are also seen as patient and kindly by others. That, too, he made clear. "Fair enough," one might say. But should one?

Reading Waller today, I am astonished by the unrelenting harshness of the portrait of teachers he sketches for his readers. I am almost equally surprised, I must say, by what I recall as being my rather uncritical acceptance of that portrayal during my initial reading. What was I thinking, I now wonder, when I read that book for the first time? Did I really believe that Waller was just reporting the facts as related to him by informants, "friendly" and "unfriendly?" I find it hard to accept my own naiveté if that is so, for it is now appallingly clear to me that Waller himself was about as unfriendly a commentator on the affairs of teachers as one can be.

I am now additionally annoyed by how clearly Waller fails to deliver on his promises. He says early on, "Where there seem to be two sides, we shall state both and leave the reader to choose for himself" (p. 381). But that's not what happens at all. Instead of offering a balanced perspective, he piles on criticism and skimps on praise. Moreover, he blithely accepts the allegations against teachers made by his unidentified but obviously "unfriendly" informants (who I begin to suspect did not exist at all) and then moves on to use those judgments as the framework of his theorizing. Instead of calling such views into question, or at least musing on why they contained so much venom, as we might expect a fair-minded social scientist to do, Waller proceeds to offer a sociological explanation for how all those negative characteristics actually come into being. He describes in some detail how the conditions within schools—organizational structure, and so forth—are responsible for producing them.

Why did I fail to detect the blatant bias of Waller's perspective during the course of my earlier reading? Or, conversely, how do I account for my belated sensitivity? To be truthful, I have no satisfactory answer to these questions save to say that I have spent a lot of time teaching, thinking about teaching, and interacting with other teachers between now and then. I also have become a closer reader of texts than I was thirty years ago. That may help to explain the difference in the two readings. Additionally, the times themselves have changed. We live today in a different world than we did then. And we share a vastly altered climate of opinion about a lot of things. But to be perfectly honest, I fear that one major reason for my overlooking the sharp edge of Waller's criticism, or provisionally excusing its excessiveness, was that his was a prejudice that at the time I partially shared. My doing so may help to explain the intensity of my negative reaction to his outlook at this late date.

In a recent interview the poet Richard Wilbur described how this process works for him. "If I denounce something in a poem," he said, "I denounce it because I understand it. And why do I understand it? I understand it because the reprehensible thing I'm pointing to is something of which I'm capable or even guilty" (Kronen, 1991, p. 45). "All satire is confession," Wilbur quotes a friend of his as saying. And so may all criticism be, I want to add.

In any event, my present confessional mood prompts me to share the basis of my belated self-diagnosis. Recall the personality profile my colleagues and I discovered, which we thought to be distinctive of teachers. Recall also how readily we made sense of its four salient features. The profile was essentially unattractive in psychological terms. In fact it conformed rather closely to a lot of what Waller said about teachers. Yet we did not look upon our findings as being at all surprising. On the contrary, they made perfect sense to us almost immediately. We had no difficulty at all coming up with a post hoc explanation that made those features seem reasonable. One that fit the facts perfectly. How shall we read that fit? Was it testimony to our ingenuity and inventiveness as explicators or was it merely that the facts confirmed what we had long suspected? I now believe the latter to have been the case.

As additional evidence of our negative bias, recall also the little ditty we went around singing to amuse each other, the one modeled on a popular tune of the day. "Ya teach sixteen years and whadaya get?" we chortled, "A little more deferent and lower in het!" Why was that so amusing at the time? And why is it still good for a laugh today? Its humor is obviously based on the fact that it pokes fun at teachers. It casts them in a bad light. It works, in other words, the way ethnic or racial jokes work. The laughter they evoke, even when the person who tells them does so in a good-humored way, is won at the expense of the group being ridiculed.

Having introduced the idea of racial prejudice, I can't help interjecting yet another quote from Waller's book. This one I also seem to have overlooked the first time through. It is a comment Waller makes in a section that treats the injustice of stereotypes, a topic that itself takes on a certain irony in light of my accusations about Waller's complicity in perpetuating a negative image of teachers. Discussing the way in which stereotypes in general imprison their victims, causing them to cry out in protest, Waller proceeds to arouses his readers' sympathies even further by pointing out that such cries of protest are "rarely heard, or rarely understood, or rarely believed." He then goes on to make the following observation:

> School teachers, like negroes and women, can never quite enter the white man's world, and they must remain partial men, except in the society of others

who, like themselves, are outcast. School teacher prejudice is as difficult a thing to combat as negro prejudice. (p. 421)

Indeed prejudice of any kind is a difficult thing to combat,
just as Waller says. It is even hard to recognize in some of
its more benign guises, as my own experience teaches.

So I now believe I have at least a partial answer to the
question of why we gave up so easily when our emerging
picture of teachers turned out to be nothing more than a
picture of the changes people go through as they age. It
seems we weren't really interested in the question of how
teaching affects teachers, at least not in any wholehearted
way, which would have made us willing to do whatever
might have been necessary to find the answer. We were
trying to answer a different question entirely, though I am
not at all sure that we knew back then what that question
was. And I doubt that even now I can frame it properly. I
think it might have been something like: Can we substan-
tiate with the use of this new and promising psychological
tool (the Edwards PPS) the image of teachers that Waller
and others depict and to which we ourselves tacitly sub-
scribe? When the answer to that question turned out to be
no, we simply threw in the towel. Our collective curiosity
did not extend to wondering about the general effects of
teaching on teachers. Is that observation intended as a
criticism of our former selves? Not really. We were doing
the best we could at the time, I suppose. Moreover, hind-
sight commonly makes us now look wiser or more sensi-
tive or whatever than we once were.

So much, then, for why we abandoned our search for
teaching effects thirty years ago. But what of now? Why
am I unwilling to pursue the query any further on my
own? The point at which my earlier effort had begun to
falter was with the recognition of my inability to distin-
guish between what teaching had done to change me and
what experience in general had done. I couldn't figure out
whether I had changed my teaching habits or they had
changed me. Without being able to make that distinction,

it seemed to me impossible to say what effect teaching has had on me. Yet having said all that, I remain convinced that being a teacher has had a profound effect on my life. It has made me what I am today or at least has had a hand in doing so. That conviction explains why I went on to say that the notion that teaching may have *no* effect on those who teach just doesn't make any sense to me. To that extent, at least, I remain in full agreement with Waller's contention about teaching's most pronounced effect being upon teachers themselves.

But therein lies a dilemma, if not a paradox. How can I remain convinced that teaching made a big difference in my life, and doubtless has done the same for teachers through the ages, without at the same time being able to specify what that difference consists of or looks like? Unless I can produce convincing evidence of teaching's effects, won't I ultimately have to concede that maybe it didn't make such a difference in my life after all? Faced with that intolerable prospect, what choice have I but to press on with my introspective search?

"The trouble is," I say to myself in a mood of mounting frustration, "though I believe the effects to be there, I am equally convinced that my looking for them won't do any good. It will lead to naught." Why so? How can I be so sure my ruminations will lead nowhere? My readiest answer is the following: Because the experiences that comprise a lifetime of doing anything—whether it be teaching, selling shoes, or being a heart surgeon—are so vast, so variable, and so inextricably intertwined with the rest of life that it is impossible to treat them as a unified causal force whose effects can be neatly or even crudely separated from the nexus of other forces that shape us as individuals.

Does that mean that it never makes sense to explore the effects of one's having been a teacher? Was I foolish to have pursued that line of inquiry for even this short a time? No, I think not. For if my hunch is correct, what is misguided about such an undertaking is not the search itself, but one's conception of its outcome. In other words, it is the kind of effects one is looking for that determines how fruitful or disappointing one's search for them will turn out to be.

So far I have been looking for a set of personal characteristics (traits, attributes, dispositions, or whatever) that could be linked by some chain of compelling logic to my experience as a teacher. That effort has proved fruitless to this point, making its continued pursuit unpromising. Yet in the face of that failure and despite the dismal outlook I refuse to give up my conviction that I owe a lot to teaching, that it has contributed significantly to my personal growth and development, and that I am a very different person than I would have been had I never taught. How shall I account for the tenacity of that conviction?

It was while pondering that question that I began to see how my introspective efforts, though worlds apart methodologically from the research tradition within which my colleagues and I worked some thirty years ago, were essentially the same as those earlier efforts in *expectation*. In both instances what was being looked for was a set of stable characteristics whose origins could be ascribed to teaching. A nearly identical framework of assumptions governed both endeavors. Its terms derive from everyday speech, though they also appear in psychology texts. There they crop up in connection with the assumption that humans are best described as possessing a set of traits, attitudes, interests, or values, whose origins and development it becomes the business of psychology to explain. That psychological framework, I finally realized, was what was getting in my way. It was the framework and not the search itself that I had to abandon.

At about the same time I also realized that the single, most obvious outcome of my career as a teacher (leaving aside specific memories for the moment) was my strong conviction that teaching had made a difference in my life. "Now *there*," I said to myself, "there is an 'effect' of teaching that I surely cannot deny." No sooner had I said that, however, than new worries arose. Did teaching really *produce* that conviction? Is it a belief that all or most teachers share? Might not such a conviction be false? Might it not be false for me?

Those questions and others like them crowded in at once. However, unlike what happened before when similar questions had stirred up a storm of doubt, the doubt this time seemed easier to dispel. For example, with respect to the question of whether teaching was actually the source of my conviction, it is clear that my having taught is at least a necessary, if not a sufficient, condition for what I believe to be so. It would make no sense for someone to say, "I am convinced that my having taught has changed me, though I have never been a teacher." Might some teachers have taught for an appreciable length of time without being convinced that the experience had changed them in some way? Possibly, though I find that hard to imagine and would certainly want to find out whether those people had ever really reflected on the question. If they said that they still remained unconvinced that the experience had changed them in any way at all (as opposed to being uncertain about *how* it had changed them), I fear I would begin to distrust their testimony, which reinforces what I have already said about the strength of my own conviction.

What about the possibility of my being wrong? Could I be *erroneously* convinced that teaching has made a difference in my life? Well, the fact of my being convinced cannot itself be in error, though I could certainly falsely testify to that effect. But as a statement about *how I stand* with respect to a proposition, my conviction is no more open to error than is any statement I make about what I believe about something. But if beliefs can be true or false, why not convictions? The answer is that not all beliefs *can* be true or false, nor can all convictions. Only those that refer to empirical assertions can be so classified. If I believe I will go to the theater tonight, my statement is not made true or false by my going or not going. This is so because it refers to the state of my expectation with respect to a future event.

With these distinctions in mind, consider now my con-

viction about the impact teaching has had on my life. Does
it rest upon an empirical claim or does it not? The way I
have talked about it so far certainly makes it sound as
though it entails a variety of empirical assertions. The use
of terms like "impact" and "effect" only add to that impression. Moreover, when I mentioned my memories of teaching and spoke of them as being among the most tangible
"evidence" of the effect teaching has had on me, I was certainly referring to something that was "real" in a psychological sense, for we commonly speak of memories as
though they were almost tangible. They can be recalled,
described, savored, lost, and so forth.

All of this implies that I believe there to be a solid, empirical underpinning to my conviction, even if I can't say
as much about it as I would like. But as empirically oriented as all that sounds (and indeed is in important ways),
I must go on to point out that my conviction about how
teaching has affected me extends beyond whatever might
be implied by those empirically oriented assertions. It includes a sense of being indebted to teaching for its having
contributed to the fullness of my life. There is a sense in
which I have no idea what I mean when I say that. For I
certainly don't know how full or how empty any other life
I might have chosen would have turned out to be. But like
Frost's traveler in "The Road Not Taken," I have a sense
that my choice of teaching "has made all the difference." I
say that not with a sigh, as did the speaker in Frost's poem,
but with fully as much conviction.

Teaching, I have come to believe, has enriched my life
in ways for which I shall always be grateful. It has caused
me to be concerned about the well-being of others in much
the same way as would a parent or a good friend, though
with rather less emotional involvement of course. It has
literally forced me to continue the pursuit of knowledge in
a formal, scholastic way long past the time when most
people leave school and lay their textbooks aside. It has
allowed me the luxury of reflection and contemplation far

beyond that afforded many who work at other jobs. It has awakened me to questions that I otherwise would probably have ignored or brushed aside, not the least of which is the very question being explored here.

That question, it turns out, has a teacherly character all its own, even though it may from time to time vex the practitioners of other occupations fully as much as it does me. After all, who cares more than teachers about the impact of experience? Moreover, one of the odd things about teaching is that it engenders doubts of various kinds, doubts about its effectiveness as a form of intervention and about how well one is doing at it. Doubts, too, about how to proceed in this or that situation and about the wisdom of past actions. From time to time those doubts turn inward and one begins to wonder, as I have been doing here, about the payoff of teaching to teachers themselves. So my uncertainty about how teaching has affected me is itself part and parcel of how teaching has affected me. Of that too I am convinced.

Let me restate the problem as it now stands. I am convinced that teaching has made a difference, a big difference in my life and at the same time I am uncertain, very uncertain, about what that difference consists of. Does that make sense? Can those two conditions coexist? My answer has been: they do. That being so, I have sought to explain how I can manage to remain convinced in the face of my uncertainty.

Having given up the search for conventional indicators of what effect teaching may have had on me, I have turned to my own sense of conviction about that state of affairs and have found there, paradoxically perhaps, some of the strongest evidence so far of the difference teaching has made. I have done the same thing, more or less, with my feelings of uncertainty. They too, at least in part, seem to be an outgrowth of my teaching experience. What it begins to look like, in other words, is that the effects of teaching, at least for this teacher, are among the conditions that

have prompted my search for them. However, instead of
lying "deep within," as I initially supposed, they have almost literally been under my nose from the start!

That discovery, if that's what to call it, prompts me to
return to a piece of "evidence" that came to mind almost
at once when I began my introspective search, though it
was just as quickly discarded. I refer to my memories of
teaching. I previously described those memories as com-
prising a kind of scrapbook of names and faces that one
might occasionally browse through at one's leisure. What
prevented me from taking them seriously, as I went on to
explain, was that they seemed too peripheral to merit consideration (insufficiently "integral" was the word I used
then). I begin now to question the wisdom of that judgment.

My memory of teaching or, a better way of putting it,
what I can remember about teaching turns out not to be a
scrapbook of images that can be leafed through at will.
That metaphor, which popped to mind almost at once
when I began to think of my teaching past, now strikes me
as being far too conventional and constrained. Rather,
what I am capable of remembering from all those years
spent in classrooms or, to put it a bit differently, what I
draw upon in the process of remembering is much more
like a vast, fluid body of material—a reservoir perhaps, or
even a city dump complete with gulls and smoldering
heaps of debris—than it is like a photo album that one
might hold on one's lap. What I dredge up from that reservoir I make use of in a variety of ways. Some of its contents
have been so often retrieved and put to use that they spring
to mind at the slightest provocation. These make up things
called "favorite stories," "funny incidents," and "fond memories." They also include countless items that function
more like pieces of knowledge or well-mastered skills than
like memories per se. I remember with ease how to do
things related to teaching (like plan a lesson) and I recall
where things are (the room I am to teach in tomorrow, for

example!). I know the looks of puzzlement or boredom on the faces of students that mean something has gone wrong instructionally. I can usually sense when it is best to drop a line of questioning and when to pursue it further. I know what it feels like when a lesson fails, and also when it succeeds. I know what it means to be criticized by one's students and how great it feels to be praised by them. I know what it's like to lose one's train of thought when responding to a student's query. I know what chalk smells like, what it feels like in the hand, what it sounds like when it moves across the board, and how its dust leaves marks on sleeves and pants.

Where does all that knowledge come from? Mostly from my experience as a teacher. And what makes it available to me? My memory does, or at least that's what I'm calling it for the time being. Earlier I wanted to dismiss that kind of knowledge as evidence of how teaching has affected me because it seemed too close to technique. Such things, I said, weren't enduring enough. They didn't reveal much of anything about my psychological make-up. I'm still of that opinion, more or less, but I am no longer put off by the threat of not getting down to psychological bedrock. Moreover, what I now see is that a list like the one I have just rattled off is but the tip of the iceberg. There is vastly more to be drawn upon from my teaching past should I choose to do so. The ease with which the items on that list sprang to mind shows that to be so.

I also see something else, which is that my sense of being a teacher and of having been one for quite some time is somehow quickened and made more concrete by the process of reflection. This is a bit unnerving, I must confess. It is almost as though I was bringing my teaching self into being before my very eyes, *realizing* it, so to speak, through my effort to find out what it is. In short, the more I think about myself as a teacher, the more teacherly I feel. And the more teacherly I feel, the more certain I am, of course, that teaching has changed me, though I remain for-

ever unsure of exactly how that change will manifest itself
in action or in my continued reflections.

What good does it do to think along these lines? What
difference does it make whether I become more aware of
how teaching has affected me or not? A quick answer to
these questions, and a truthful one as well, is that I find it
personally rewarding to reflect on my past in this way. It
seems to me perfectly consonant with the ancient Socratic
adage: Know thyself. And one hardly need apologize for
following *that* advice.

But that answer is not entirely satisfactory for it
doesn't cover two related questions that were put to me by
a sympathetic critic with whom I was discussing this project before it was very far along. "Even if it is helpful or
enjoyable to you," the critic began, "what is to prevent an
exercise like this from being dismissed as sentimental and
self-indulgent? In short, why should anyone but you want
to read it?" Those two questions hit home for me because I
have raised them myself in connection with the recent
trend toward encouraging classroom teachers to keep
journals and write autobiographies. I have no dispute with
those who would prompt teachers to engage in such prac-
tices. In fact, I am confident that for many teachers the
writing of diaries and the keeping of journals would prove
to be very worthwhile. But I do wonder sometimes when I
run across long excerpts from such personal accounts in a
professional journal or a text on teaching what anyone but
their authors is supposed to get out of them. That question
is one I must now address with reference to what is being
written here.

What originally stirred me to add this chapter to the
book was the realization that the question of how teaching
affects teachers is a natural extension—actually, a sort of
mirror image—of the larger and more important question
of how teaching affects students. The latter, of course, is
what the preceding three chapters sought to explore. To
balance that outlook, it made sense, I thought, to step
through the mirror. Having now done so, I am struck by

how complementary the two perspectives are, how each reinforces the other while at the same time contributing something of its own to an understanding of the effects of schooling upon all who attend, teachers and students alike.

What both perspectives reveal at a very practical level, it seems to me, is the shortsightedness of restricting our consideration of the outcomes of schooling to measures of academic achievement, however fancy their dress, a practice all too common, I fear, among today's researchers, professional educators, and the public at large. At the same time, all that has been said here does little to buttress the hope of our correcting that shortsightedness by adding even fancier assessment procedures to those already in use, a proposed solution that one hears much talk of these days. What is needed much more than new measures of scholastic attainment, it seems to me, is a new way of thinking about what our schools are seeking to accomplish, or perhaps what is called for is the revival of some older ways of thinking about what our schools are for, I am not entirely sure which is the better way of putting it. To explain my uncertainty on this point I need to return to a consideration of the features shared by the two outlooks that have been presented.

To begin, both the student's and the teacher's perspectives instantiate a fairly common human experience that is encapsulated in the familiar feeling of having been profoundly affected by somebody or something without being able to say precisely what the effects are or how they came about. Such was the situation that led to my reveries about Mrs. Henzi and that motivated the narrator in Kinnell's poem, "The Schoolhouse." A similar kind of awareness was at work in my introspective reflections, though there the focus was on the potency of a way of life rather than a single individual.

An alternative version of this common experience is that of waking up to the fact of one's reacting to the world in a certain way or possessing a certain characteristic

82

Untaught Lessons

without knowing how or when that happened. Emerson (1983 [1844]) gives voice to the latter version of the dilemma in his essay, "Experience," where he remarks:

> All our days are so unprofitable while they pass, that 'tis wonderful where or when we ever got anything of this which we call wisdom, poetry, virtue. We never got it on any dated calendar day. Some heavenly days must have been intercalated somewhere. . . . (p. 471)

Heavenly days, indeed. Such are the explanations we seem almost forced to accept when we start from an understanding of what we are like now (or what we think we are like) and try to move backwards in search of causes. But why should that be so? Why must we wind up relying on heaven-sent miracles to explain how we came to be as we are? If my own introspective efforts can be relied upon for at least a part of the answer to that question, it is that the causal forces seem too numerous and too impossibly entangled ever to be sorted out satisfactorily.

Wordsworth, another literary figure who pondered such matters deeply, frames the question rhetorically in a memorable passage of *The Prelude* (1979 [1850]) where he asks:

> But who shall parcel out
> His intellect by geometric rules,
> Split like a province into round and square?
> Who knows the individual hour in which
> His habits were first sown even as a seed?
> Who that shall point as with a wand, and say
> 'This portion of the river of my mind
> Came from yon fountain'? (II, lines 243–249)

The answer that Wordsworth wants from his readers is clear enough. He wants them to say "no one" to all three of his questions. Yet the irony is that he himself spent years pondering those rhetorical conundrums, or ones very much like them, and in the process produced one of the greatest poems in the English language. As his most recent biographer, Stephen Gill (1990), puts it, "That Wordsworth knew no certainty could be achieved did not stop him searching. . . . The river, Wordsworth knew, had its origin somewhere" (p. 13). Well, maybe. At least Wordsworth wrote as though he thought it did, which may be all we need to acknowledge at this point. Moreover, he ultimately succeeded in answering his unanswerable questions, at least to his own satisfaction. Or perhaps it would be better to say he put them to rest. For that may be all we can do with questions of this kind. We answer them temporarily, or we give up trying to do so for the time being because we simply run out of steam or other matters intrude upon us or for some other reason, and then we return to them with renewed energy at some later date. That's what seems to have happened to the narrator in the Kinnell poem treated in Chapter 2. It also characterizes my own thoughts about Mrs. Henzi and my reflections on what I observed in Mrs. Martin's room.

Is this any different than what happens throughout life? Aren't we always abandoning projects before they are finished and then returning to them later on when it is more convenient to do so or when we find ourselves in a more suitable mood? Clearly so. But there is an important difference between the kind of reflective pondering under discussion here and the vast majority of the unfinished and interrupted tasks that crowd our days.

Thoughts about what brought us to where we are today, which was Wordsworth's topic, or about what we owe our former teachers, which has been the guiding query throughout most of this book, are different in at least two ways from many of the other vexations we recurrently ponder. First of all, they don't have answers that can be verified by checking them against some external reality as do many other questions. In short, there is no way to prove that one's answers to such questions are correct. Secondly, although little, if anything, of a practical nature turns on the answers we give to them, these kinds of questions seem unusually important all the same. They nag. One keeps returning to them, almost against one's will. They are, in a word, haunting, or can become so to those possessed by them. What makes these questions so compelling, I believe, is that in our answering them what hangs in the balance is not just the answer to the specific question we happen to be pondering. Rather the ultimate outcome of such thinking is the kind of person we want to be or the kind of life we want to lead. In short, we define ourselves and our way of life at least in part by the thought we give to questions of this kind, the things we think about in the lulls between life's more pressing events. Moreover, that observation holds true, it seems to me, as much for our professional selves and our ways of acting on the job as it does for our life in general. The kinds of teachers and students we are or want to become owe as much in all likelihood to what we think of during our solitary moments as to the things said and done in class or during periods of formal study outside of school.

Returning to the narrower focus of the specific question that concerns us here, we may profit in ways other than those already mentioned, it seems to me, from the insights of literary figures like Emerson and Wordsworth. As both of those men surely knew, and as we have seen in these pages as well, the sheer complexity of the task is not the only explanation of our inability to say much about where our traits and characteristics come from. Another piece of the answer, one whose revelation to me personally owes more to my recent observations in classrooms than to reflections on my own experience as a student or a teacher, takes into account the temporal dimension of such changes. That accounting reminds us that the outcome of repeated exposure to a set of conditions that might ultimately produce enduring effects (a condition such as sitting in the same classroom for weeks on end) occurs so gradually that the amount of change that takes place daily or even weekly is indiscernible, and therefore the process as a whole goes unnoticed. The truth of that observation has important implications for where and how we look for the causes of change. It requires that we narrow our vision and humble it as well. The narrowing allows us to focus on features of the environment that we might ordinarily pass by—small details and minuscule events, happenings that come and go in a twinkling. The humbling, which goes hand in hand with the narrowing, turns us toward the ordinary and mundane and away from the dramatic and colorful.

These two shifts of orientation that point us, as observers, toward the minute and the mundane, resemble, of course, the angle of vision that characterized the Romantic poets and their successors during the nineteenth century. "To see a World in a Grain of Sand/ And a Heaven in a Wild Flower," as did Blake (1927, p. 188), or to note that "the meanest flower that blows can give/ Thoughts that do often lie too deep for tears" as did Wordsworth (1983, p. 302), is to observe minutely and humbly.

But as those scant lines also make clear, the Romantics did more than look closely and affectionately at the world around them. They constantly sought to look past that world or through it, to see beyond the surface meaning of things. They strove to "read" their surroundings much as one might read a complicated text or a piece of scripture. Lovers of nature they certainly were, but they also worshipped the human imagination, whose power to envision more than the eye alone could behold was looked upon as the ultimate source of artistic achievement.

This interpretive or hermeneutical orientation within the Romantic worldview, which expressed itself as the urge to delve beneath the surface and to ferret out hidden meaning, is also something from which teachers and others who look upon the educational scene have much to learn. For the significance of what goes on in classrooms, and what we discover when we turn our thoughts to our former teachers or to memories from our own experience as teachers or students, resides less in the immediacy of what we see or remember than in what our observations and remembrances come to stand for, what they lead us to appreciate and acknowledge. If not the world in a grain of sand or heaven in a wild flower, we who teach must at least learn to see the interest that lies behind a look of attentiveness, the sullen weariness that resides in the silence following a question addressed to the class as a whole, the tension that fairly crackles through the classroom during the taking of a test, the eagerness expressed by the sudden thrust of an upraised arm. And those, of course, are only the most obvious of the detailed, interpretive readings that teachers are constantly called upon to make as they go about their daily work. There are also interpretive puzzles for after hours: the question of what to make of an enigmatic response from an otherwise straightforward student, the wonder about the significance of a casual remark that could signal the onset of a dramatic change of attitude, the worry about whether the student who always sits in the furthest corner of the room is trying to say something through his physical location that he lacks the courage or insight to put into words. These situations, too, call for a reading that looks beyond the surface of classroom life.

There is a danger, however, in drawing this comparison between the Romantics and the needs of today's educators (as I see them). For it may sound to some (particularly to those with scant knowledge of the Romantics or a strong bias against them) as though what is being advocated here amounts to a kind of fuzzy-minded, mawkish sentimentality toward students and teaching, which stands in the way of clear thought and leads to the sort of mush that constitutes the worst of what is written and said about teachers and teaching. In addressing that danger I must first point out that nothing being said here prevents one from seeing the negative side of teaching and schooling. A close and reflective look at what goes on in schools or at the impact of one's prior experience as a student or teacher can certainly reveal much that is regrettable, undesirable, and perhaps even painful. Indeed, it would be odd if such were not the case. As the old humorous adage reminds us—Romantic idealism notwithstanding—little drops of water and little grains of sand can also make mud. Moreover, the aptness of that observation is as applicable to what can be seen in classrooms as it is to the world at large. There is plenty of mud in schools should we wish to go looking for it.

At the same time, I must acknowledge that the point of view taken here is indeed slanted toward a positive and optimistic reading of educational affairs (rather than a negative and pessimistic one). It is so, in part, because such a point of view comes naturally to anyone who has anything to do with education. Why is that so? Why should we educators be more inclined toward optimism than anyone else? The answer, in a nutshell, is because our work calls for it. Because education is fundamentally an optimistic endeavor. It is grounded in hope. The entire educational enterprise rests on the conviction that improvement is possible, that knowledge can replace ignorance, that skills can be learned. Moreover, its practitioners not only view those changes as possible, they are committed to bringing them about. They also intrinsically value them. They honor those who achieve them. Education is by definition future oriented, which provides yet another reason for it being infused by a spirit of optimism. It offers the promise of a better life to those it serves. Its supporters and practitioners, or at least those among them who have given the matter sufficient thought, envision a society enriched by the services they render. Absent these and other assumptions that flow from the nature of education as a human activity and teaching itself would make no sense at all.

The positive outlook of educators may not be necessary in a logical sense. One can imagine (though with some difficulty, it seems to me) a despairing teacher, one who carries on his or her work though burdened with a deep sense of its futility. However, one would certainly not wish to be that person, and even less his or her student.

This positive bias calls for caution, for it means, among other things, that the danger of excessive sentimentality is indeed a real one and must be guarded against, despite what has just been said about there being plenty of room for a negative perspective on schooling for those inclined to a less-than-optimistic outlook. The risk of becoming Pollyannish seems small, however, when placed beside the corresponding risks of cynicism and despair that attend the opposite point of view. But what about neutrality? Why not look upon teaching and all that goes on in schools and classrooms with a neutral eye? Why not adopt an attitude of detached neutrality? Wouldn't that be the scientific way? It would be if one were trying to be objective in the way that science dictates. But objectivity of a scientific kind is precisely the wrong orientation to take with respect to the kind of questions under examination here. What is wanted instead is something more like a kindly bias, a forgiving eye, an attitude of appreciation, a way of looking that promotes the growth of sympathetic understanding.

Here is another way of thinking about it, one that brings us almost full circle to where this chapter began. The question of how teaching affects teachers, as I have belatedly discovered in the process of writing this chapter, is by no means the same as the question of how one's life as a teacher had affected one. Nor is an inquiry into how teachers influence their students the same as asking how one of our own teachers, like a Mrs. Henzi or the snaggle-toothed master of Kinnell's one-room school, may have influenced you or me. The two sets of questions—one general and quasi-scientific, the other deeply personal—are obviously related to one another. Indeed, they look to be so intimately connected in a quasi-logical sense that one might expect their answers to at least overlap. Thus, if we knew all there was to know about how teaching left its mark on teachers, it would seem as though we would also have the answer to the question of how our own teaching has influenced us. The same with the pair of questions about teachers influencing their students. Reversing the situation, if we teachers all knew for certain how we had been shaped by our own teaching, it would seem as though we already possessed the answer to the broader question that concerns teachers in general. This also applies to the teacher–student relationship. These apparent linkages are deceptive, however, for they do not take into account the possibility that what seem to be similar questions are really quite different. Moreover, what makes them so is not just that within each of the pairs one question deals with a single individual and the other with a group of people, although that is certainly true. They differ, however, in a variety of other ways as well—in the occasion that calls them forth, in the motives that undergird them, in the terms in which their answers are framed. When I asked what effect teaching has on teachers, for example, as I believed myself to be doing those many years ago, I was searching for regularities that I hoped would hold true for many or most teachers. When I turn, however, to the question of how teaching has affected my life, what I am looking for is something entirely different. I am seeking an answer *that feels right* to me, that makes intuitive sense, that coheres in a way that is personally convincing and therefore satisfying, that jibes with my prior convictions, my memories, my sentiments, my knowledge of what has happened to others, my current understanding of how occupations leave their marks on us all, and more. This is not to say that I may not be surprised by the answer I come to, and consequently be forced to alter some of what I had previously believed, but it does imply that such changes take place within an ongoing interpretive system and are not simply a matter of exchanging ignorance for knowledge or replacing one belief with another. What changes is one's outlook on life or one's worldview. The situation is equally complex, of course, when I start thinking about one of my former teachers and what I learned from him or her beyond the lessons in the textbook or curriculum guide.

Here, then, is where my journey ends, almost where it began, although I seem to have traversed quite a distance from start to finish. What has my wandering revealed about what effect teachers and teaching have on us? Noth-

ing that can be reduced to a law or a principle, that's for
sure. Not even a textbookish generalization of the kind
that might be taught to teachers in training. But it has left
me (and I hope my readers) more convinced than ever that
our teachers do affect us in profound and unfathomable
ways and that one's being a teacher can and often does
leave one changed for life even though the more important
of those changes may be far from obvious. More importantly, perhaps, it has brought to light a jumble of consid-
erations that bear upon the process of thinking about such
matters.

Chief among them is the suggestion that we educators
might with profit look to the Romantics for help in coming
to grips with those outcomes of schooling that have to date
so eluded our nation's test-makers and pollsters. If we
want to know how schools and teachers are really affecting
our students, this view tells us, we must learn to look with
a keen eye at the minutiae of classroom life. There, if we
look closely enough and do so sympathetically, we may begin to appreciate the benefits of schooling as never before.
We may also become more acutely aware of what needs to
be changed to increase those benefits.

Many of our most memorable teachers, like Mrs.
Henzi, Mrs. Martin, and the shadowy figure of Galway
Kinnell's poem, probably don't need this advice. They already know where and how to look to see more than meets
the eye in their classrooms. Indeed, some of them, like Mrs.
Henzi, seem to have an extra pair of eyes in the back of
their head! However, those of us who presently lack that
kind of vision need not despair. With practice and the help
of those who have led the way in opening the eyes of generations past—Wordsworth and Emerson being two of my
own favorites, but scores of other artists and poets are no
less valuable as guides—we may cultivate a heightened
sensitivity to the nuances of schooling, not only for ourselves but for our students as well. An increased ability to
discern and to appreciate the untaught lessons that
schooling delivers cannot but benefit us all.

Epilogue

As I explained at the beginning of the last chapter, the notion of exploring a fourth perspective on the influence of teachers, one that would focus on the influence teaching might have on teachers themselves, occurred to me too late to be accomplished within the time available for the preparation of the initial series of Sachs lectures. I nonetheless resolved to address that perspective in a separate essay when I returned to Chicago. Though I was not quite sure how that piece would turn out, I thought it might serve well as the concluding chapter of this book.

Because I was no longer constrained by the necessity of keeping the fourth essay short enough to be delivered as a single lecture, it wound up being considerably longer than the other three, far too long to be publicly presented. What I had not anticipated at the time of its writing was that it too would wind up being presented before a public audience. When President Timpane of Teachers College learned that I had written a fourth essay to accompany the other three, he kindly invited me to deliver a version of it as the fourth and final lecture in the series I had presented the previous fall. To comply with his request, I prepared a briefer version of the longer piece, though one whose contents closely mirrored those of the original. There were, however, a couple of significant changes.

First of all, in the presented version I placed somewhat

more emphasis than I had in the last chapter on the importance of memory in coming to grips with the question of
how my own teaching may have affected or may yet affect
me and, by indirection, with the broader question of how
their own teaching may have affected or may yet affect
other teachers. The odd phrasing, with its "may have af-
fecteds" and "may yet affects," signifies a process in which
outcomes are not only dimly understood, more to be sur-
mised than known for certain, but radically unfinished; a
process, in other words, in which past and present commingle, one whose outcomes are continually capable of
coming into being, of being realized.

   In the speech itself I made use of the distinction
between diachronic and synchronic conceptions of time,
drawing on the work of Gadamer, Ricoeur, and others.
Diachronic time, which is the same as clock time and the
time physical scientists use, is one in which past, present,
and future events occupy hermetically isolated time seg-
ments with the only possibility of interaction being that of
physical causality, which operates in one direction only.
Synchronic time is that in which past, present, and future
events commingle and affect one another. It is, one might
say, *cultural* time, the temporal framework in which our
interpretation of complex cultural objects, such as works
of literature and art, take place. Within that framework,
past events, such as the beginning of a story we have read
or the opening bars of a symphony we are listening to, continue to acquire new meaning as the work unfolds. Even
though they are past events in diachronic time, they continue to color one's understanding of what is taking place
in the present and of what the future might hold. The future, in its turn, already exists within such works, in the
sense of already having been written or made, although
that future, diachronically present, is only gradually dis-
closed to the interpreter or viewer. Its ultimate disclosure
sometimes causes one to revise one's understanding of
both the present and the past.

   This synchronous intermingling of past, present, and

future is precisely what happens, I argued, when one reflects on one's prior teaching experience and tries to figure out what one has learned from it or what remains to be learned. In this sense, then, one's teaching past remains an active force in one's life or can become one through a process of reflection, rumination, and imaginative reconstruction. It is a plastic force as well, in that it is susceptible to change through reinterpretation. We change our minds about our teaching past (as I did in the process of writing the last chapter) and in so doing we re-create it. We also surprise ourselves from time to time by dredging up memories that have long been dormant, for so long sometimes that they may even seem brand new. In this way we continue to refurbish the past, to *realize* it, one might say. Thus, in my fourth and final Sachs lecture I sought to convince the teachers in the audience, of which there seemed to be quite a few, that continuing to think about their teaching past, to mull it over and to try to make sense of it, was a good thing to do.

I also came up with a different ending to my remarks than the one that brought the last chapter to a close, an ending that seemed to me better suited to the spirit of the occasion than the one I had written earlier. Here is the ending I used:

Where has my excursion into the effects of my having been a teacher taken me? It has left me more convinced than ever that teaching has made a difference in my life, though not the kind of difference that I had set about looking for. I have certainly failed to uncover a set of traits or characteristics that I can unequivocally attribute to my years of teaching. Teaching has affected me, it would seem, the way being married has done, or being a parent, or being a Midwesterner for most of my adult life. I don't mean to equate those different kinds of experiences, except to maintain that each has contributed in profound and yet-to-be-fathomed ways to the person I am today.

I retain memories of teaching, as one might expect, but

except for a couple of stories that I have told many times about a year I spent teaching a special class in New Jersey (my very first year of teaching, as a matter of fact), those memories are oddly fragmented and much scantier than one might imagine. They are certainly not the Hollywood-ish, nodding-by-the-fire reveries of a Mr. Chips. Nor are they the full-blown tales of the raconteur. They are more like the raw stuff from which memories worthy of relating to others might someday be made, the bricks and mortar from which such tales could be artfully constructed if one had the talent and were keen on doing that sort of thing.

I feel grateful for having been a teacher. I have enjoyed the life it has made possible. I am speaking here not of the privileges that have gone with being a university professor (though I have certainly enjoyed those as well), but of the day-to-day pleasures of teaching and of working with students.

I have a hunch (can it ever be more than that?) that I am not only a different person than I would have been had I never taught, but a better person as well. In short, I think teaching has improved me. It has done so, if my hunch is right, by requiring me to perform a role that by custom entails a host of moral obligations. There is no guarantee, of course, that the performance of such obligations leaves in its wake an improved performer. But if Aristotle is right (and he often is), there is no better way to instill virtue and make it habitual than by insisting that a person act virtuously. Teaching, as I have experienced it, gives one plenty of opportunity to act the part of the virtuous person.

I think if I were to portray my teaching experience as a visual work of art it would have to be an abstraction—a collage perhaps, or, better yet, something like a cubist painting by Braque or Picasso. It would contain references to a number of the physical and psychological invariants of classroom life and would do so through the use of visual icons, those shapes and colors so common to classrooms as to be universally understood. You know the ones I mean— pieces of chalk, a felt eraser, a smeared blackboard (and a clean one, too), a cluster of chairs, a pile of books, raised hands, attentive faces, pads, notebooks, pencils, the ubiquitous clock on the back wall, a closed door, a mottled ceiling with fluorescent lights, as well as the windows that look out on the scene beyond—a scene that the poet John Malcolm Brinnin in his "Views from Favorite Colleges" refers to as "the exiled blossoming world," and fragments of that world as well, they, too, would have to be included—a patch of sky perhaps, the outline of a tree, a Gothic tower in the distance. I wouldn't be in the picture myself, of course, except maybe as a hand, writing on the board, or as the tips of a pair of men's shoes, which is where I often concentrate my gaze when trying to think of an answer to a student's question.

As for colors, Braque's grays and browns and forest greens would be far too somber, I fear. So would the colors Picasso typically used during his cubist period. As a matter of fact, I have just realized that the size of the cubist paintings (at least the ones I have seen) wouldn't do, either. Far too small, you see. I would need a canvas at least the size of a regular blackboard, one covering the entire side of a fairly large room. Floor to ceiling, perhaps. The dimensions of a Rauschenberg. That would be more like it.

Back to the palette. I'm not sure what colors should dominate but there would be a lot of bright green and white. Apple green for today's blackboard (and youth). White for chalk (and hope). Perhaps the entire canvas should have a canary yellow undercoating, like the walls and ceilings of most of the classrooms in which I have taught. But there would have to be some brighter yellow as well, bright bars the color of Van Gogh's sunflowers, to stand for the shafts of sunlight that cut diagonally across the room in the late afternoon, promising an end to the day's labor. Those same yellow shafts could double as symbols of intellectual illumination, of light breaking through darkness. And of course there would have to be brown, the brown of desktops, grained like oak and scarred by initials here and there. And red, we would need red somewhere, even though I am not sure what red would be doing in a classroom. Maybe it's a visual pun. Yes, that's it. It stands for being "well read," which is what a teacher hopes to be and what he hopes for his students as well. And gray, too. We mustn't forget gray, the color of ignorance, uncertainty, and doubt. Those negative conditions must have a place in the picture, too, although not an overpowering one. Perhaps the gray could be made to resemble gray hair so that it could stand for wisdom and ignorance at one and the same time. I find that possibility attractive for obvious reasons.

Well, as you can see from this visual fantasy, I'd not be much of a painter, sad to say. My picture would be far too derivative and hackneyed. To me it brings to mind one of those murals that high school students are forever painting on the far wall of the school's cafeteria. A worthwhile project from an educational standpoint, no doubt, but hardly noteworthy as a work of art. The same would be said of my own effort, I am sure, were I ever to act on my fantasy.

No matter. I haven't been paid all these years to paint pictures. What I've been paid to do has been to teach. And that I've done to the best of my ability (most of the time). How has teaching affected me? I've told you some of it. The rest I leave to your imagination and my own, though I frankly think that yours would be much better spent trying to figure out how teaching and/or teachers have affected *you*. If these brief exercises in doing just that have managed to move some of your thoughts in parallel directions, I shall have accomplished what I set out to do.

References

Abrams, M. H. (1984). *The correspondent breeze*. New York: W. W. Norton.

Blake, W. (1927). In G. Keynes, (Ed.). *Poetry and prose*. New York: Random House.

Cavell, S. (1976). *Must we mean what we say?* Cambridge: Cambridge University Press.

Cavell, S. (1979). *The claim of reason*. New York: Oxford University Press.

de Man, P. (1983 [1971]). *Blindness and insight*. Minneapolis: University of Minnesota Press.

Dewey, J. (1929). *The quest for certainty*. New York: G. P. Putnam's Sons.

Emerson, R. W. (1983 [1844]). *Essays and lectures*. New York: Library of America.

Fischer, M. (1989). *Stanley Cavell and literary skepticism*. Chicago: University of Chicago Press.

Gill, S. (1990). *William Wordsworth, A life*. Oxford: Oxford University Press.

Hume, D. (1969 [1739]). *A treatise of human nature*. London: Penguin.

Kinnell, G. (1982). *Selected poems*. Boston: Houghton Mifflin.

Kronen, S. (1991, May/June) [Interview with Richard Wilbur.] *American Poetry Review, 20*(5), pp. 45–56.

Waller, W. (1932). *The sociology of teaching*. New York: John Wiley & Sons.

Webster's New International Dictionary (2nd ed.). (1937). New York: Merriam.

Wittgenstein, L. (1972 [1921]). *Logisch-philosophische Abhand-lung.* New York: Humanities Press.

Wordsworth, W. (1979 [1850]). *The prelude, 1799, 1805, 1850.* New York: W. W. Norton.

Wordsworth, W. (1983 [1807]). *The Norton anthology of poetry* (3rd ed.). New York: W. W. Norton.

Yeats, W. B. (1973). *The Norton anthology of modern poetry.* New York: W. W. Norton.

Index

About the Author

Philip W. Jackson is the David Lee Shillinglaw Distinguished Service Professor in the Departments of Education and Psychology and the Committee on Ideas and Methods at the University of Chicago. He holds a Ph.D. from Teachers College, Columbia University, and is a member of the National Academy of Education. He served as President of the American Educational Research Association in 1989–90. In addition to *Untaught Lessons*, he is the author of *Life in Classrooms* (Teachers College Press, 1990), and co-author, with J. W. Getzels, of *Creativity and Intelligence.*